The Girls' Super Activity Book

ARCTURUS

ARCTURUS
This edition published in 2013 by Arcturus Publishing Limited
26/27 Bickels Yard, 151–153 Bermondsey Street,
London SE1 3HA

ISBN: 978-1-78212-060-5
CH002597EN

Written by Lisa Miles
Designed by Jeni Child
Illustrated by Robyn Neild
Edited by Becca Clunes

Printed in China

Supplier 23, Date 0213, Print Run 2175

Contents

Follow the girls on a trip full of adventures! Along the way, there are hundreds of fun puzzles, cool quizzes, drawing ideas, things to make and MORE!

CRAFT ACTIVITIES
Don't forget to ask an adult for help with scissors!

Meet the girls!

The girls are going on a trip together!
Find out who's in the gang...

TAYLOR

Taylor is full of fun and she LOVES music and dancing. She likes discovering new places to go, especially if she can take her friends!

Mini file

Best activity: dancing and music
Top outfit: denim shorts and T-shirt
Loves to wear: purple

Mini file

Best activity: swimming
Top outfit: surf top and board shorts
Loves to wear: blue

ANNA

Anna is the one who gets the girls together and arranges all the fun. Nothing gets in her way and she's always in a sunny mood!

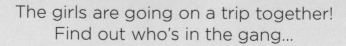

CARLA

Carla loves animals and one of her best hobbies is horse riding. She's always kind to her friends and ready to help them out if she can!

Mini file

Best activity: looking after animals
Top outfit: anything with horses on it!
Loves to wear: green

MILLY

Milly loves being creative, from art and music to writing and cooking, and she especially loves making food for her friends!

Mini file

Best activity: cooking
Top outfit: cute dress and sunhat
Loves to wear: orange

ROXY

When it comes to style, Roxy knows best. She loves giving fashion advice to her friends and shopping for bargains is her perfect pastime!

Mini file

Best activity: shopping for clothes
Top outfit: jeans and a cool jacket
Loves to wear: pink

JESS

You can rely on Jess to take on a challenge. She loves to get outdoors and have an adventure, whatever the weather!

Mini file

Best activity: outdoor sports
Top outfit: sporty shorts and T-shirt
Loves to wear: red

Hooray, we're there!

Taylor is so excited! She's going to go on a trip for a whole week. Unscramble the letters to find out who Taylor is going with...

SETB DRENFIS

Best Friends

Find it!

Taylor's backpack is hiding in this chapter. It looks like this...

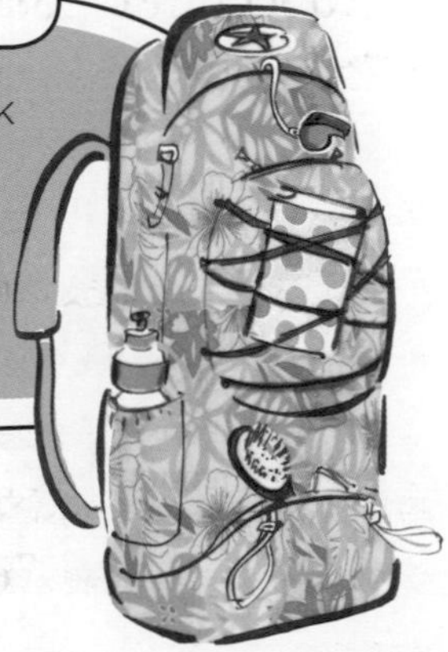

Taylor's trip

PART 1

Taylor's parents have taken the girls on a trip for a whole week. They can't wait to start having fun...

The girls arrived at Lake Truly Resort: their home for a whole week! They felt so lucky. Taylor's dad collected the keys to their cabin and they settled in straight away. There were so many things to do at the resort. There was an exercise studio, a games room, a café and a water park, plus loads of activities in the local area. It was a perfect place for the girls to enjoy themselves!

Anna wanted to start exploring, but Taylor had another mission on her mind. She grabbed the resort brochure and flopped down on an enormous sofa. She flipped through until she got to the activities section and ran her finger down the list.

"Great! Just as I thought, there are dance classes every morning. I'm going to book myself in. Who wants to join me?"

"Let me have a look," Jess said. Taylor held out the brochure but as she did so a printed leaflet fell out from between the pages. Anna picked it up and read it aloud.

DEAR GUESTS
There will be no dance classes this week because our dance teacher is unwell. We are sorry for any inconvenience.
Jane Forrest,
Activities Manager

"But that's SO disappointing. My trip is ruined!" Taylor exclaimed and ran to her room.

"Poor Taylor, what shall we do?" said Milly.

"Let's try and think of something," Anna replied.

A short while later, Anna knocked on Taylor's door and entered.

"I'm sorry about the dance classes," she said, "but we've got a new plan."

"Really?" Taylor looked up. She was unconvinced.

"Every day, we're going to take it in turns to arrange a really fun activity."

"That sounds OK," said Taylor a little more happily.

Just then, Taylor's mother popped her head around the door.

"Cheer up, there's a disco on tonight! Come on, let's find your best outfits!" The two girls grinned. It was a deal!

Continued on page 26...

Puzzle parade

Which picture of Taylor is the odd one out?

1

2

3

Cross out all the letters that appear twice. The remaining letters spell out something to do with the girls' trip.

B F L I T F E

A R K R I B T

Write the answer here

lake

Complete the grid so that every row, column and square contains each of these four symbols:

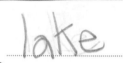

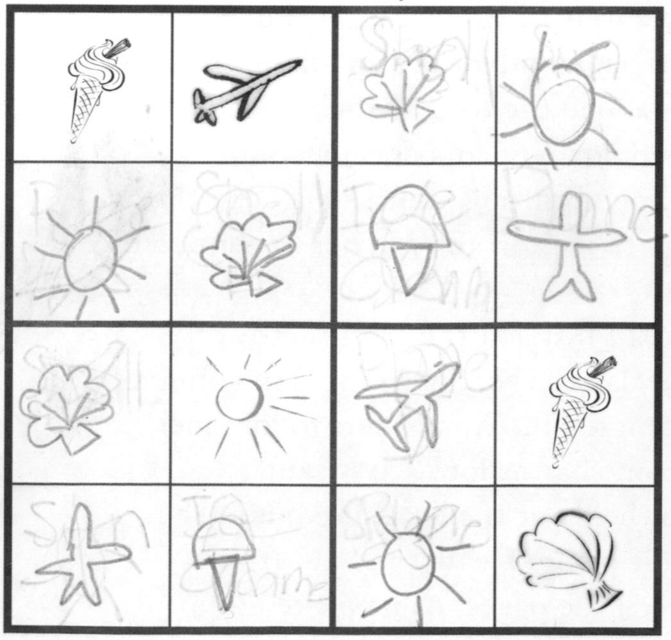

Map doodle!

Doodle your ideal destination for
an exciting trip on this map!

Is it by the beach?

Is it far away?

Add all the things you'd like to find!

Fill it in!

What's the best place you've EVER been to?

Howie

Spot the difference

There are ten tricky differences between these two pictures of the girls at their cabin. Circle them when you've found them.

A

B

What's your totally top trip?

Read these questions and circle your answers. Read the results to find out YOUR best destination for a trip away.

1 Your best way to travel is...

A. by luxury plane
B. by super-fast train
C. by comfortable car

2 Your bag-packing style is...

A. don't worry, you can buy stuff when you get there!
B. lay out all your things and select matching outfits
C. write a sensible list and stick to it

3 Your ideal book to take on a trip is called...

A. Mystery at Seashell Sands
B. Adventure in Sunrise City
C. Journey Through Wilderness Wood

4 Your one essential item for a trip is...

A. a swimsuit
B. a camera
C. a water bottle

5 You check the weather report and it looks like rain. Do you...

A. yell that you're not going!
B. check the guidebook to find indoor activities
C. pack an umbrella and go!

6 At the last minute, you throw into your suitcase an extra pair of...

A. glitzy sunglasses
B. cool shoes
C. warm socks

Read your results!

Mostly As
BEACH BABE
Your best trip is a sun-soaked stay at a luxurious beach resort. Don't forget your sunscreen!

Mostly Bs
CITY GIRL
You would love to go to a city and see all the famous sights. Don't forget your map!

Mostly Cs
HAPPY CAMPER
You love the outdoors and a tent is your ideal place to stay. Don't forget your sleeping bag!

Unpack your bag!

Taylor has unpacked but she can't find her purse. Help her track it down!

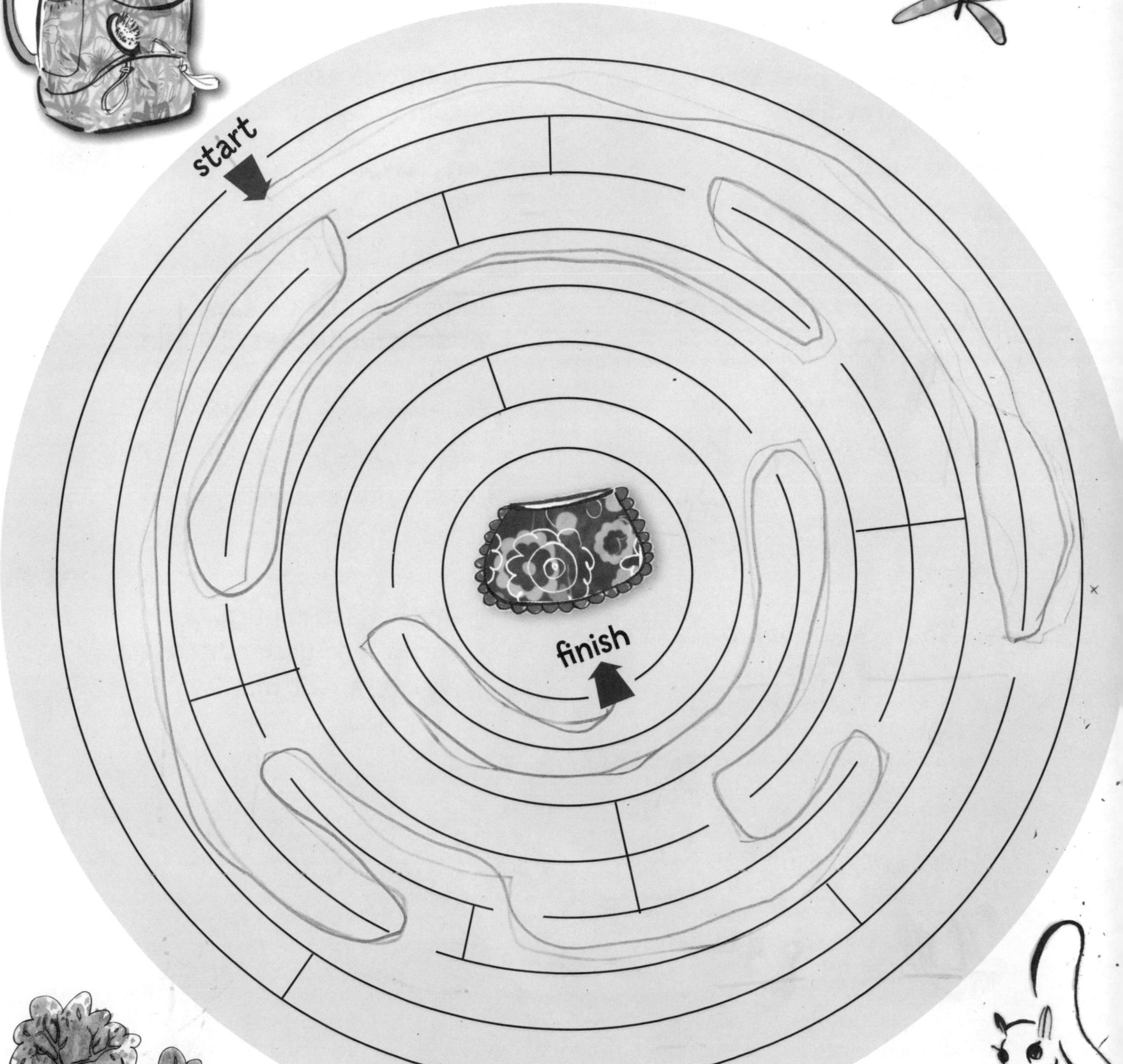

Puzzle parade

Which shadow matches the key to Taylor's cabin?

1

2

3

Unscramble the letters to reveal something that Taylor loves to do.

CINDANG

Write the answer here:

Dancing

There are four differences between these pictures of Taylor's party shoes. Find them!

1

2

Find the words!

These words are all to do with going on a trip. Find them in the grid. Look up, down, backwards, across and diagonally.

Word list

beach	forest	park
cabin	hotel	mountain
campsite	journey	relaxing
city	lake	tent

B	S	H	O	T	E	L	Y	H	E	T	K
E	C	A	M	P	S	I	T	E	U	R	H
A	R	R	O	C	P	R	U	X	H	T	F
C	E	G	A	T	K	E	Y	B	H	E	P
H	L	Y	T	L	K	K	R	A	P	N	R
B	A	K	I	N	E	E	L	T	H	T	O
C	X	H	O	C	K	T	S	E	R	O	F
N	I	N	I	Y	A	S	L	O	V	H	I
I	N	V	Y	S	L	E	T	E	H	B	N
B	G	T	O	C	S	E	Y	H	U	H	G
A	I	A	M	O	U	N	T	A	I	N	X
C	G	N	I	Y	E	N	R	U	O	J	A

Draw Taylor!

Copy Taylor's picture into the grid, square by square.

TAYLOR'S FASHION TIP
Tie a pretty, contrasting ribbon around a summer hat!

Fill it in!

What kind of hat would YOU love to wear?

Beanie

Cabin search

It's the first day of the trip and Taylor has forgotten the way back to her cabin. She knows it has a dark roof and three trees outside. Help her find it. Then take her to the lake where Anna is waiting for her!

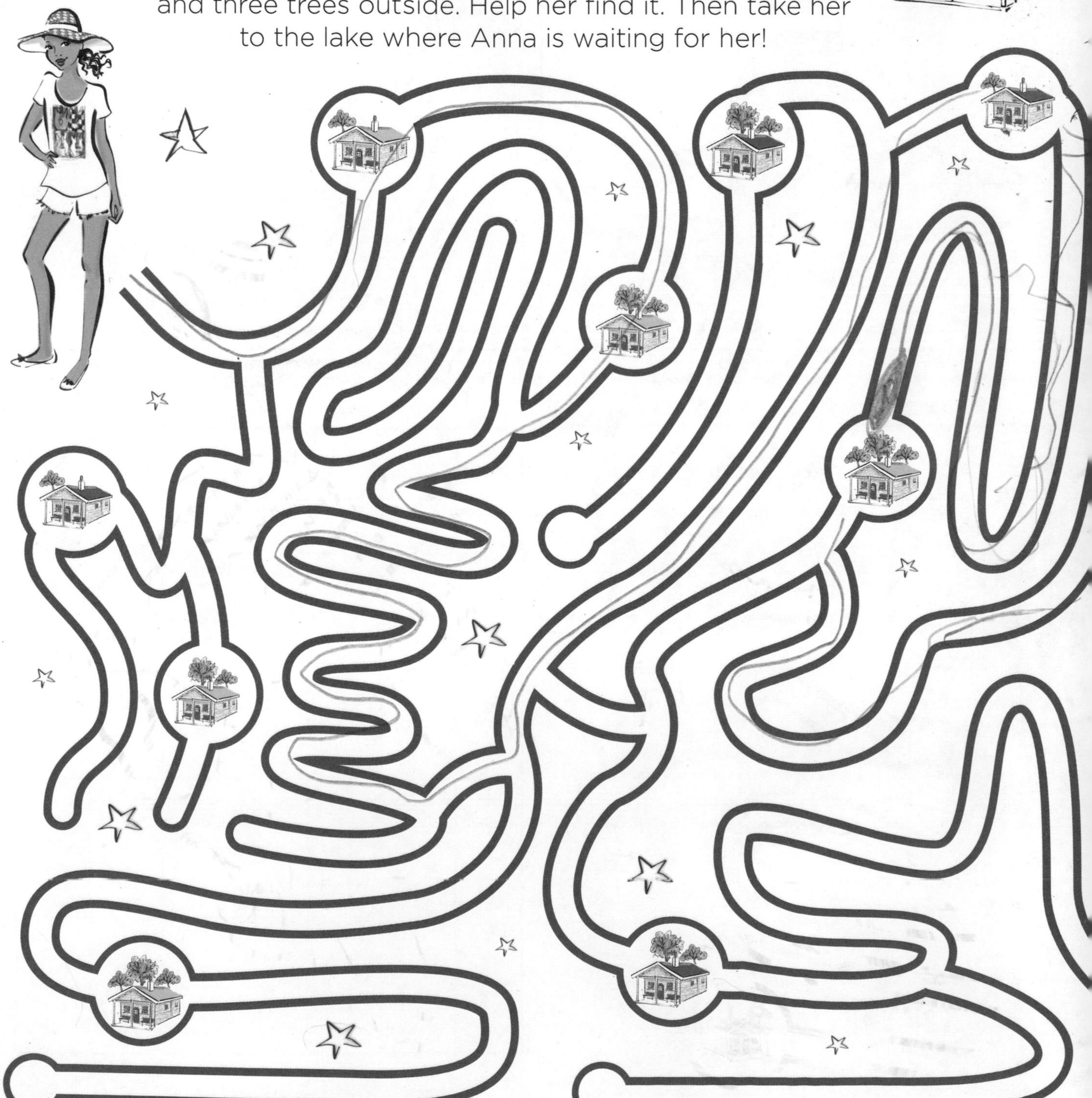

Taylor's top fashion

Add pretty shades and patterns to make an outfit for Taylor to wear on her trip.

Try a logo on the sweatshirt!

Pick a pattern for the skirt!

Make the boots a fun shade!

Puzzle parade

Which pretty hairband does Taylor wear to the disco?

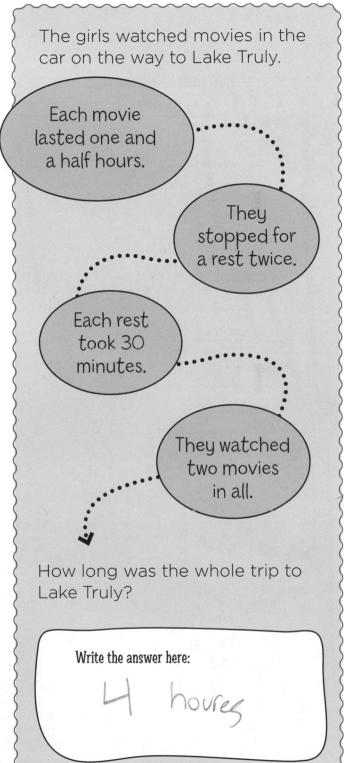

The girls watched movies in the car on the way to Lake Truly.

Each movie lasted one and a half hours.

They stopped for a rest twice.

Each rest took 30 minutes.

They watched two movies in all.

How long was the whole trip to Lake Truly?

Write the answer here:

4 houres

Room with a view

Taylor loves the view from the cabin window! What can she see?

Boats on the lake?
Birds in the trees?
Flowers on the lawn?

Taylor's diary

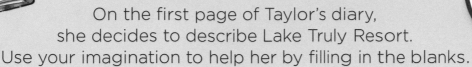

On the first page of Taylor's diary, she decides to describe Lake Truly Resort. Use your imagination to help her by filling in the blanks.

Saturday

When we arrived the weather was hot . We found our cabin and inside there was a cawsh Pool . The girls thought it was So Amazing !

We unpacked and ran off to explore the Beach . There are loads of things to do here. We can go Swimming hikeing or even CamPant ! And I can't wait to see the mauntins .

In the café, I ordered Pizza and Shake and the resort store sells my best kind of Chlocat and slushies.

I think this place is Awesome and we're going to have a Super time!

Fill it in!

What's the first thing YOU would do at a resort?

go Swimming ore the SPa

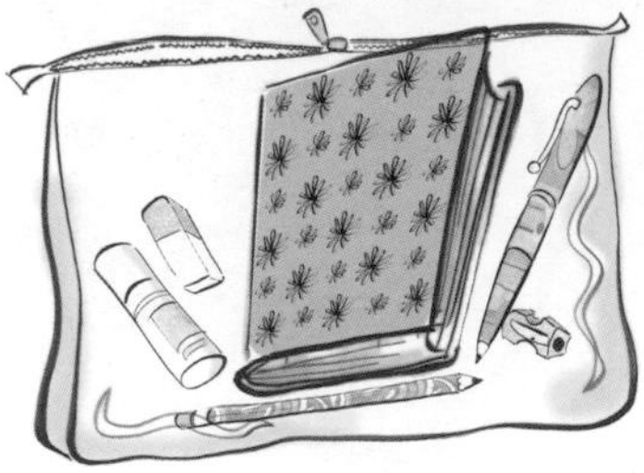

Travel journal kit

Don't wait until you get home to write your travel journal! Carry this handy kit in your backpack and record your trip as you go along.

You will need

- ⁎ Letter size plastic zip-up wallet
- ⁎ Pocket size blank hardback notebook
- ⁎ Pens and pencils
- ⁎ Eraser
- ⁎ Pencil sharpener
- ⁎ Stick of glue

1. Take the plastic wallet and put the other pieces of the kit inside it. Don't overfill it with pens and pencils, as you will only need a few.
2. On each day of your trip, write the date at the top of a new page and write your location.
3. Collect souvenirs of your day, such as travel tickets, postcards and leaflets from tourist attractions. Keep them in the wallet.
4. When you have a quiet moment, such as when you're sitting in a café or on the train, stick your souvenirs in your journal, make a sketch or write about your experiences.

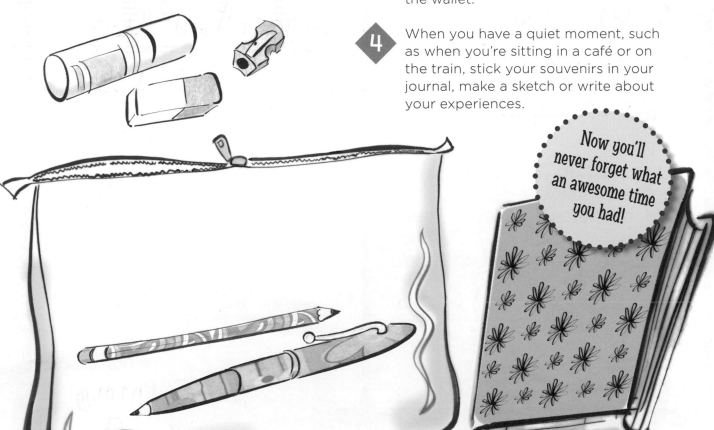

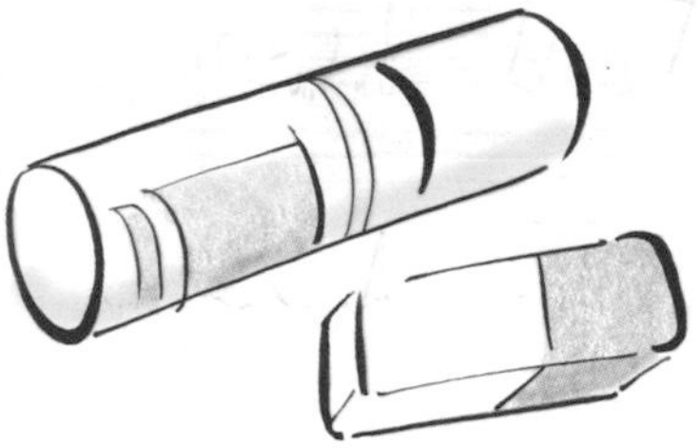

Now you'll never forget what an awesome time you had!

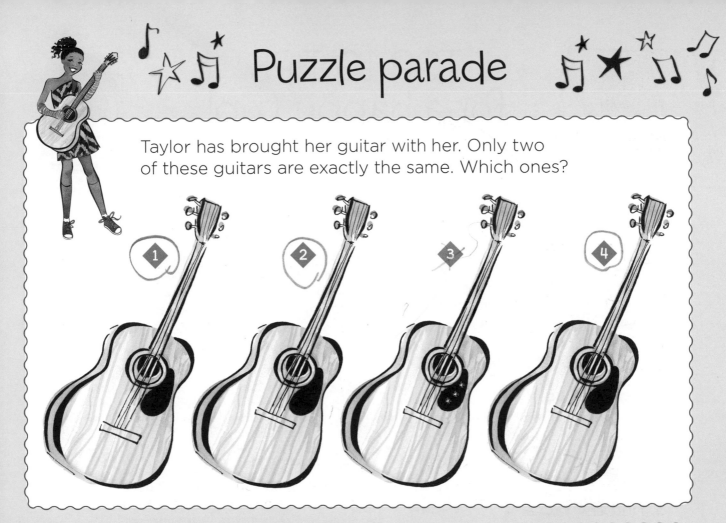

Puzzle parade

Taylor has brought her guitar with her. Only two of these guitars are exactly the same. Which ones?

How many words can you make out of the letters in the words LAKE TRULY?

....	....
....	....
....	....
....	....
....	....
....	....
....	....
....	....

1-5
Keep going and find some more!

6-10
Not bad but there's more to find!

11-16
Great, you're just the best!

TOP 10 TIPS for a happy trip!

Everyone looks forward to going on a trip. So here are ten top tips to help you make the most of it!

1. Friend or foe?

Choose your travel companions well. You'll probably be going with your family, so you'll be used to each other's ways. But if you are taking a friend, make sure it's someone who you get on with, even when they (or you!) are being annoying.

2. Get excited!

A trip is a special treat, so you're bound to be looking forward to it. Mark it on your calendar and cross off the days as it gets closer!

3. Find the facts

When you've chosen your destination, find out as much about it as you can by looking it up on the internet (get an adult's permission first) and in guidebooks. That way, you can discover what there is to do when you get there.

4. Make an itinerary

When you've done your research, make a list of things you want to do and plan when you might be able to do them. This kind of list is called an itinerary and it will help your trip run smoothly.

5. Pack wisely

Depending on where you are going, you might need to take certain items, such as your swimsuit or boots. Make a list and pack a few days before you go to make sure you don't forget anything.

6. On your way...

You might have a long journey ahead of you. Take something to pass the time, such as books, magazines or travel games. Pack them in a bag where you can reach them.

7. Be adventurous!

At your destination, there may be new activities, different surroundings or the people might speak a foreign language. Be brave and try something new!

8. Take a journal

You won't want to forget all the exciting things you've been doing so take a notebook and write a travel journal. See page 22 for a great idea on how to do this.

9. Special souvenir

A good way to remember your trip is to buy a special souvenir. It could be something simple like postcards of the places you visited or perhaps an object that you can only buy in that part of the world.

10. Don't forget...

Just like at home, stay safe when you are on your trip. Always let an adult know where you are and follow any rules. And above all, enjoy yourself: this could be the trip of a lifetime!

Water park fun!

Anna loves being in the water. Unscramble the letters on the right to find something that Anna always takes with her on a trip.

GWISMINM GBA

Write the answer here:

Swimming Bag

Find it!

Anna's best swimsuit is hiding somewhere in this chapter. It looks like this...

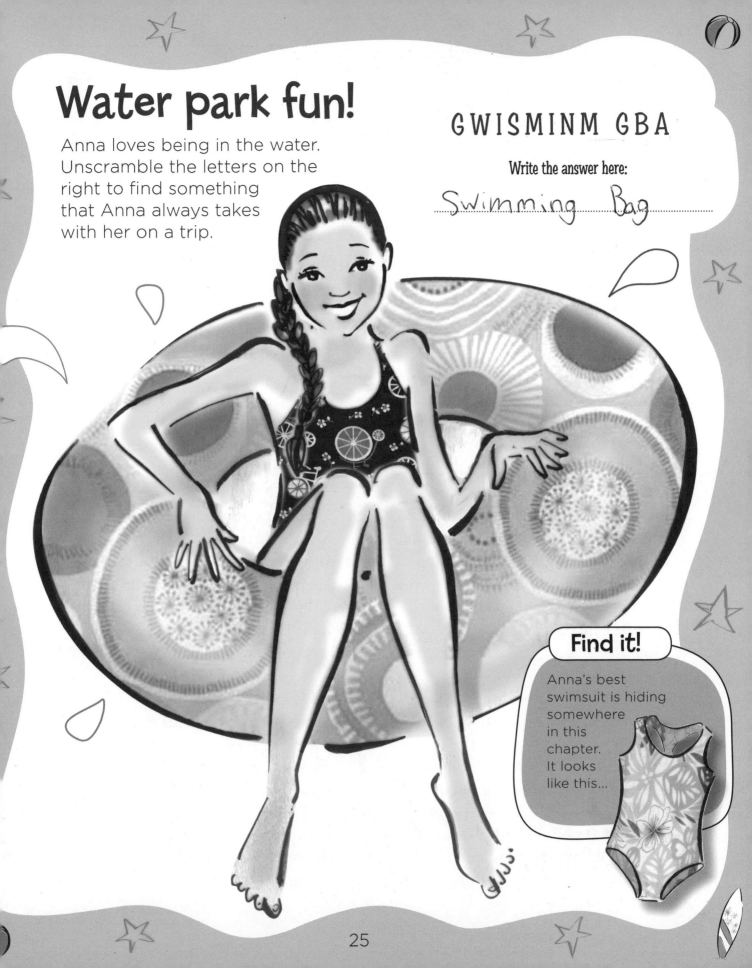

Taylor's trip

PART 2
Continued from page 7...

Anna is the first of Taylor's friends to plan a day out for the girls. Will Taylor enjoy it?

"The disco was great last night, wasn't it?" said Roxy the next morning. They nodded, all except Taylor. Last night, she'd been the star of the show dancing to all the latest songs, but now she was sad again.

"I should be at my dance class this morning," she sighed.

"We promised to cheer you up," said Anna. "It's a beautiful day, so let's make the most of it and go to the water park. Come on, let's grab our stuff!"

The water park was down by the lake. There were water slides, whirlpools and water jets, as well as a big swimming pool. After splashing around for a while, Anna suggested that they all go on the giant water slide.

"Great idea," said Carla, "let's all go down together!"

"Er, I think I'll just watch," answered Taylor.

As her friends swam off to the slide, Taylor sat on the edge of the pool and pondered. She WAS having fun but there was a problem. She was scared of going down the water slide. Taylor just couldn't pluck up the courage to join in.

Suddenly there was a splashing sound as Anna emerged from under the water and grinned.

"You coming?" she asked.

Taylor shook her head.

"Why not? It's fun," Anna continued. Then she noticed the look on Taylor's face. "Are you scared?"

"Well... just a bit," Taylor replied. "I've never been on a big water slide before."

Anna smiled. "Don't you remember the first time you danced on stage? You were really nervous then."

"Yes... but..."

"But now you love dancing on stage!" Anna interrupted. "There's a first time for everything, so why not give the water slide a try? You might love it!"

Taylor suddenly made up her mind. "OK, but only if you go with me!"

"No problem!" Anna answered.

Five minutes later, all six girls were zooming down the giant slide, making a massive splash. And even Taylor was absolutely loving it!

Continued on page 50...

Pool doodle

What do you love to play with in the pool?
Doodle it!

Is it a fun float?

Is it a big rubber ring?

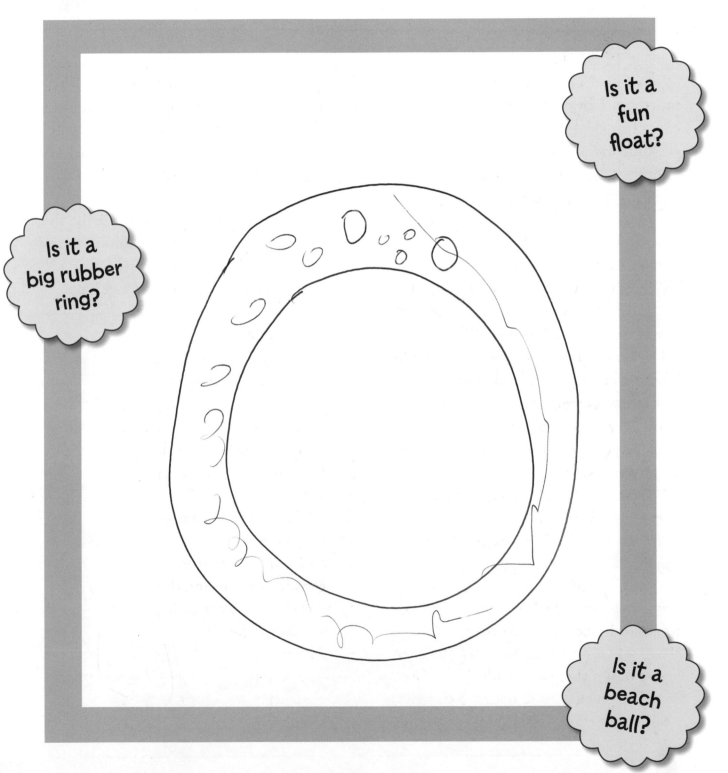

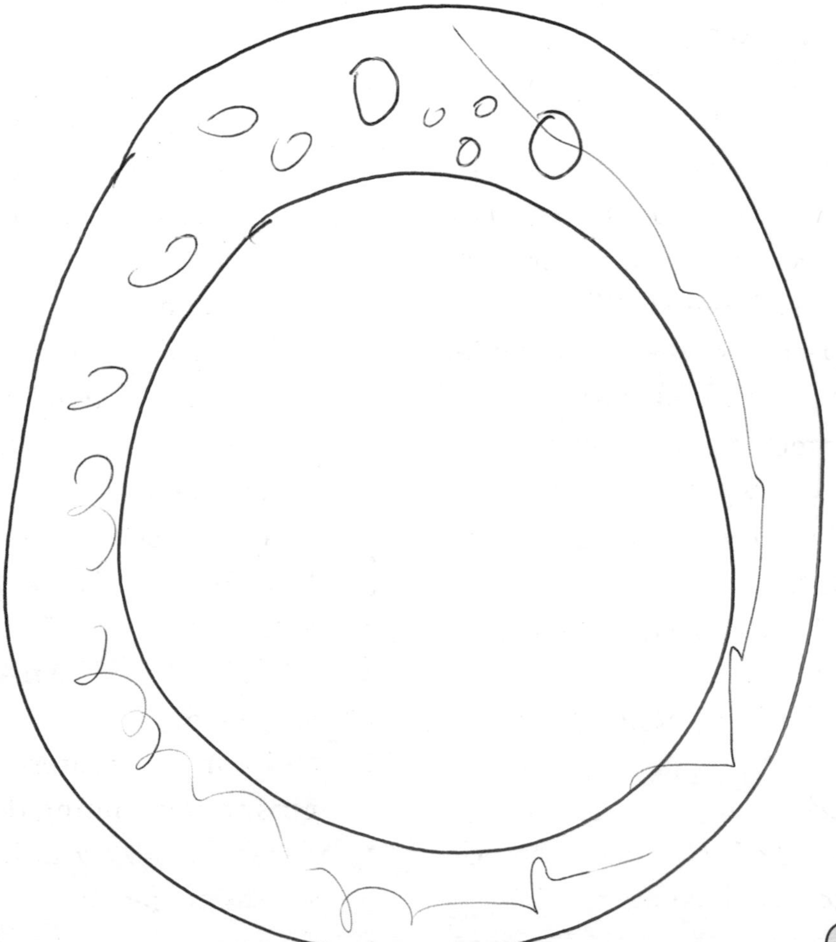

Is it a beach ball?

Spot the difference

There are ten tricky differences between these two pictures of the girls playing in the pool. Ring them when you've found them!

A

B

Are you a water wonder?

Read these questions and circle your answers.
Check the panel to find out how many points you scored and discover your swimming style!

1 **A friend suggests going swimming. Do you...**

A. grab your swimming bag and shout "let's go!"

B. check the pool timetable

C. invent a cold and say you can't go

2 **Your best swimming stroke is...**

A. front crawl because you enjoy the speed

B. butterfly because you love the challenge

C. on your back (that is, back on the poolside)

3 **Your friends are playing in the pool. Do you...**

A. dive under and do a handstand

B. swim away when they aren't looking

C. suggest a game of water volleyball

4 **Your best thing to do in the pool is...**

A. swim the length of the pool gracefully

B. execute a perfect dive from the diving board

C. whizz down the water slide

5 **On the water slide, do you...**

A. scream all the way down with sheer excitement

B. close your eyes and hope for the best

C. always go with a friend for fun

Add up your points:

1.	A = 3 points	B = 2 points	C = 1 point
2.	A = 2 point	B = 3 points	C = 1 points
3.	A = 2 points	B = 1 point	C = 3 points
4.	A = 1 point	B = 3 points	C = 2 points
5.	A = 3 points	B = 1 point	C = 2 points

5-8 points

LAND LOVER

Instead of splashing around, you'd rather relax on the poolside. Much more enjoyable!

9-11 points

WATER BABY

You love swimming and you'll always be ready with your swimming bag for a trip to the pool!

12-15 points

WATER WONDER

Amazing! You're a real water whizz kid and you're competitive, too. Set your sights on a gold medal!

Puzzle parade

Only two pictures of Anna are exactly the same. Which two?

Circle the words that CAN'T be made out of the letters in WATER PARKS.

SPARK

SWIPE

WHISK

SPLAT

STAR

TAP

SPLASH

WALK

WRAPS

Spot three differences between these two pictures of Anna's swimming bag.

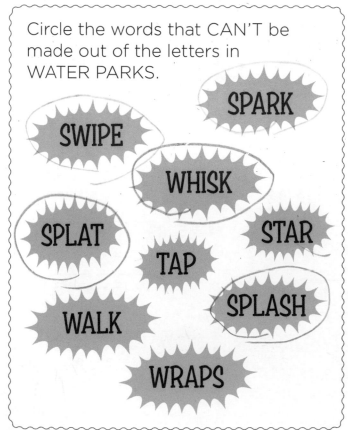

Water slide!

Take Anna down the water slide to make a big splash at the end!

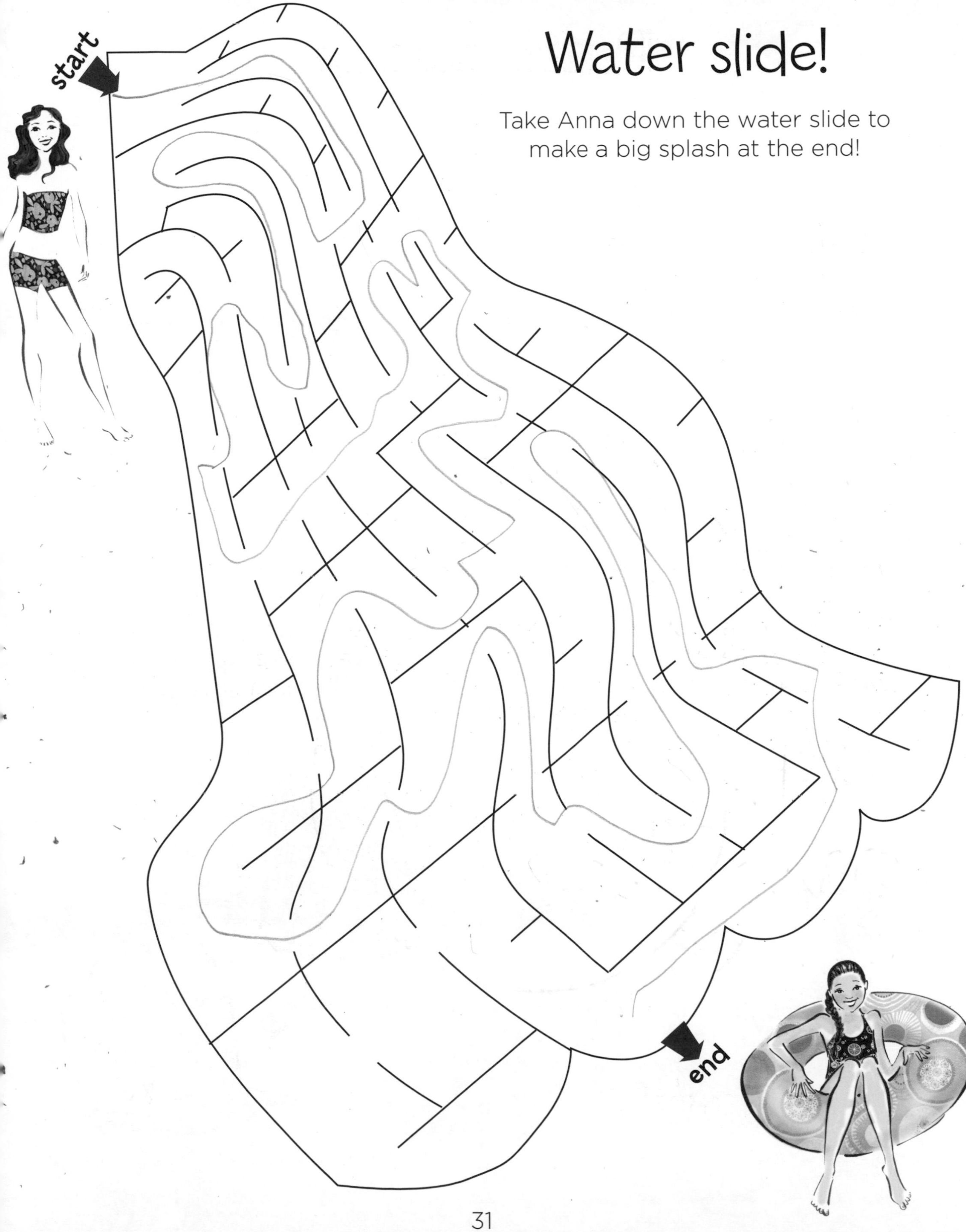

Puzzle parade

Anna loves watersports. How many can you think of? Here's a couple of easy ones to start...

sailing

swimming

Diving

tubing

water sking

wake boarding

Wind Surfing

fishing

aqua fit

canoing

Syncronize swimming

water Polo

The girls had a great day at the water park. But how long did they actually spend in the water?

They get to the park at 10:15am

It takes 15 minutes to change

They have lunch and rest from 12:30 till 2pm

In the afternoon, they get out for an ice cream for 15 minutes

It takes 15 minutes to change again and they leave at 4pm

Write the answer here:

3h 30m

Draw Anna!

Copy Anna's picture into the grid square by square.

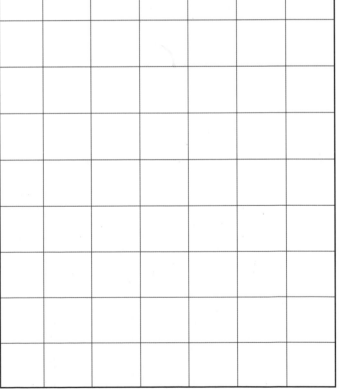

ANNA'S FASHION TIP
White T-shirts go with everything. Make sure you have one!

Fill it in!

What's YOUR best T-shirt?

....

....

Make a chooser

Anna and the girls each chose an activity for one day of their trip. If you and your friends don't know what to do today, make a paper chooser to help you out!

1 Take a square piece of paper, at least 6 x 6 inches (15 x 15cm). Fold it in half diagonally, both ways. Then fold in half vertically and horizontally. Open out after each fold.

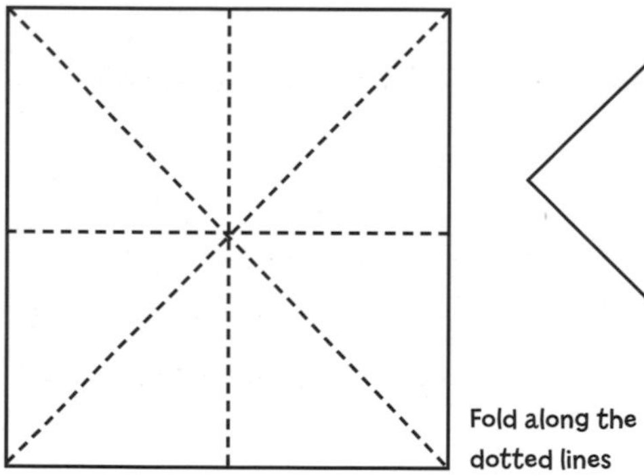

2 Fold in each corner to meet in the middle.

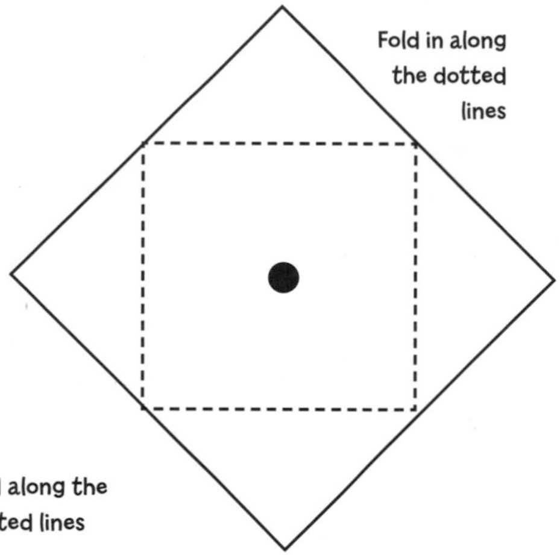

3 Turn the paper over. Write a different activity on each of the eight triangles, then fold each corner into the middle again.

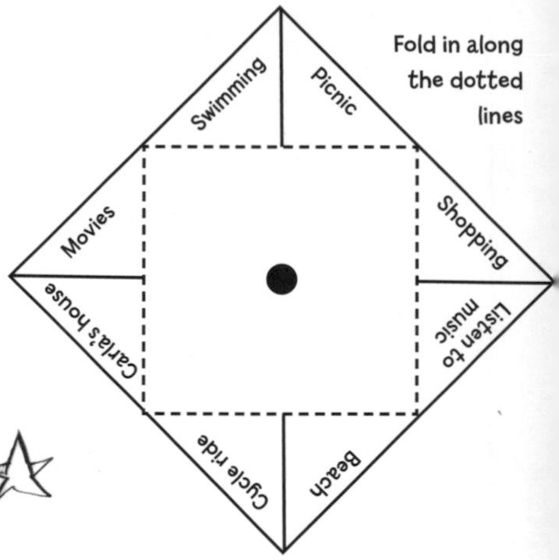

4 Write the numbers 1 through to 8 on each of the eight small triangles that are now on top of the paper.

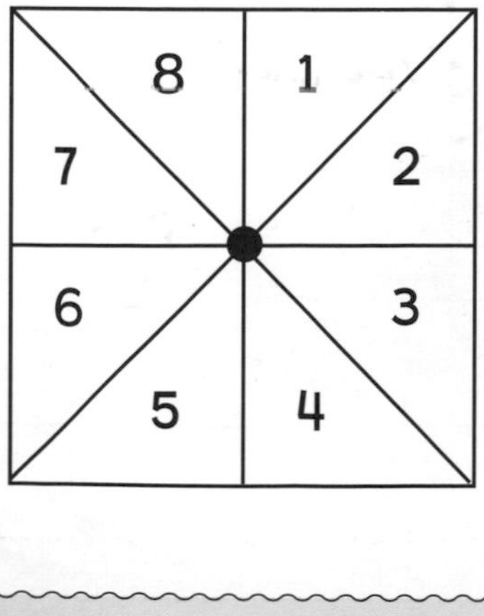

5 Now fold the paper in half from right to left, so that the flaps are open on the right.

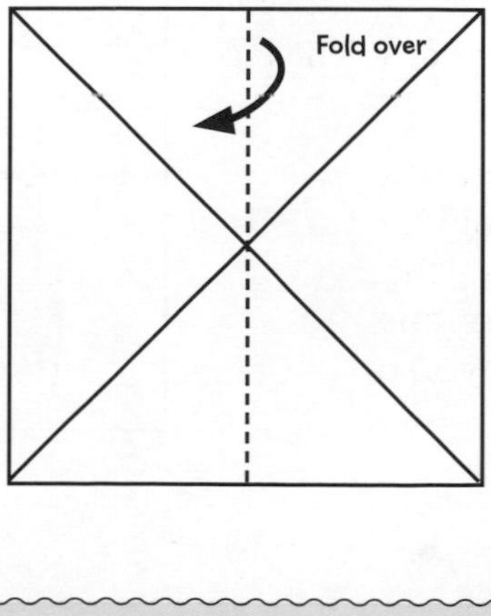

6 Turn the paper around so that it's positioned horizontally, with the open flaps along the bottom edge.

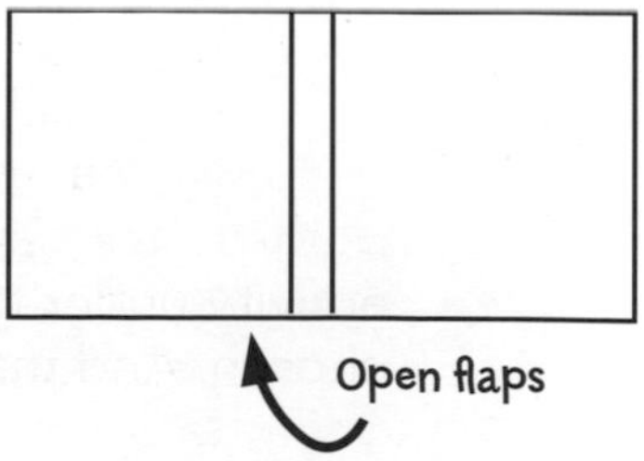

7 Slip your thumbs and forefingers under the open flaps and open and close the chooser like a bird's beak. Do this backward and forward and from side to side.

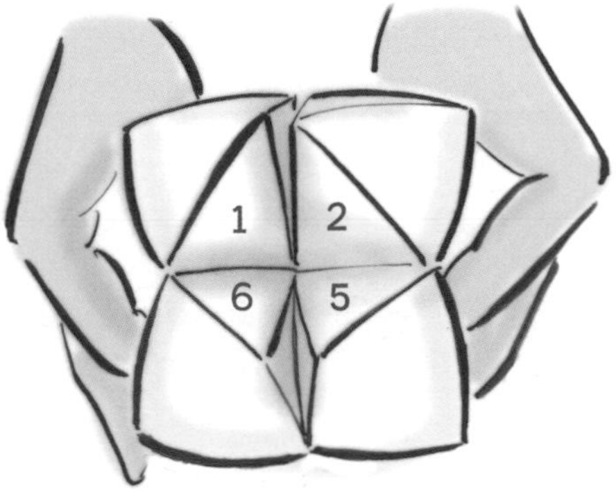

8 Close the chooser and now write on the name of four different shades on the top triangles.

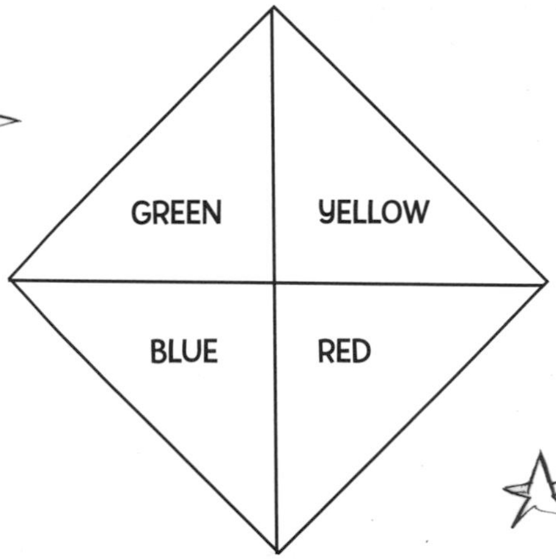

Now make a choice!

1 Hold the chooser so that the point is closed. Ask a friend to pick a shade from the top.

2 Spell out the word aloud, opening and closing the chooser each time you say a letter, for instance Y-E-L-L-O-W. Take it in turns to open it backward and forward and from side to side.

3 On the last move, hold the chooser open and ask your friend to pick a number from inside. Repeat step 2, this time counting out the number, for instance, 1-2-3-4-5-6.

4 On the last move, ask your friend to pick a final number. This time, open up the flap and read the activity under the number she has chosen. And that's what you're going to do today!

FORTUNE TELLER

You can also use this as a fortune teller. Instead of writing activities in step 3, write silly fortunes to make your friends laugh!

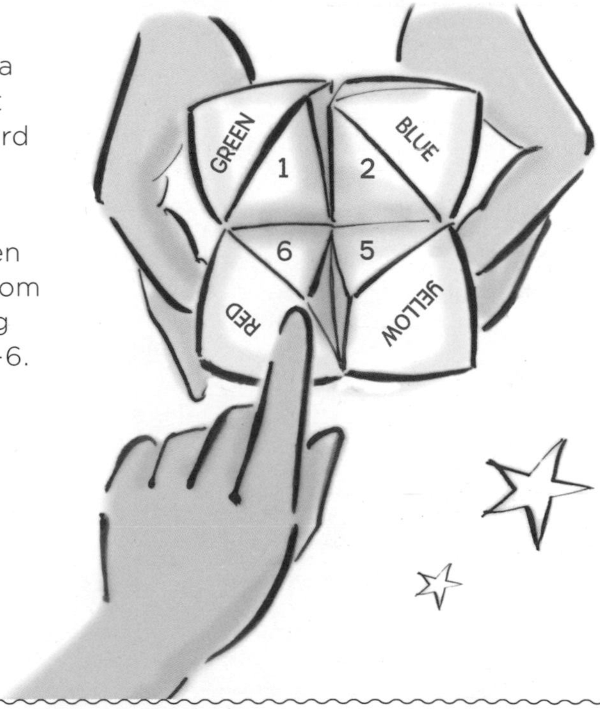

In the swim

Follow the alphabet code below to work out an important message from Anna.

The code

A = 1 B = 2 C = 3 D = 4 E = 5 and so on...

12 5 1 18 14 9 14 7 20 15

19 23 9 13 11 5 5 16 19 25 15 21

19 1 6 5 9 14 20 8 5

23 1 20 5 18

Tip
Write down the whole alphabet in code before you start!

Write the answer here:

learning to Swim Keep

Safe in the water

Swimming checklist!

Anna wrote a list of everything she wanted to put in her swimming bag for the day at the water park. Look at her list and mark off the items she's found. Which items are still missing?

Puzzle parade

Which shadow matches the picture of Anna exactly?

Help Anna find the two pieces of her swimsuit!

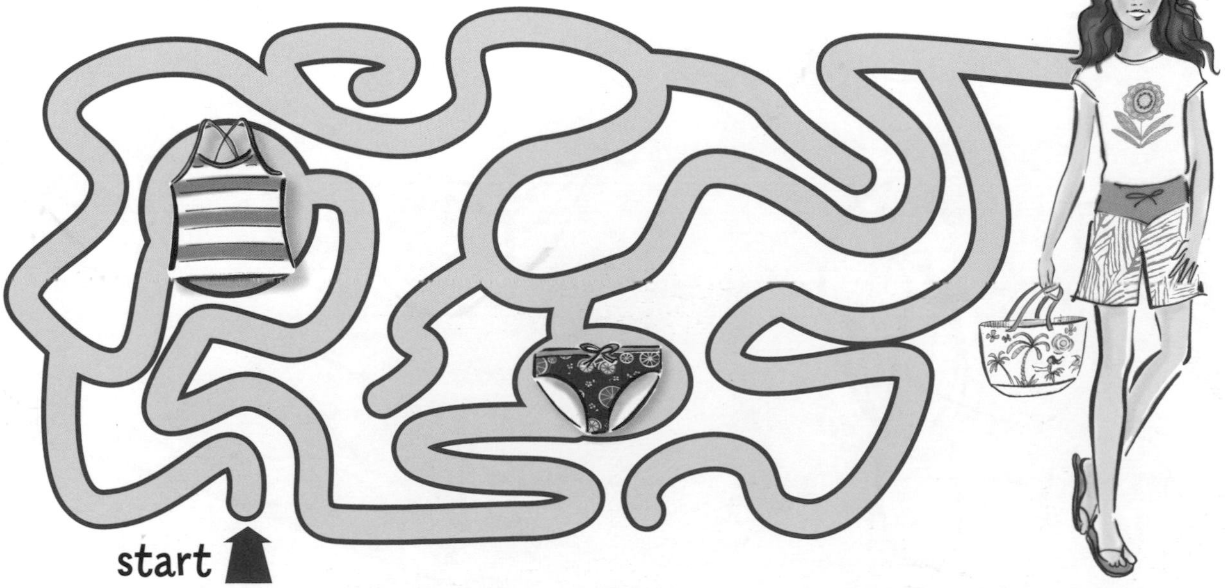

Anna's top fashion

Add pretty shades and patterns to make outfits for Anna to wear on her trip.

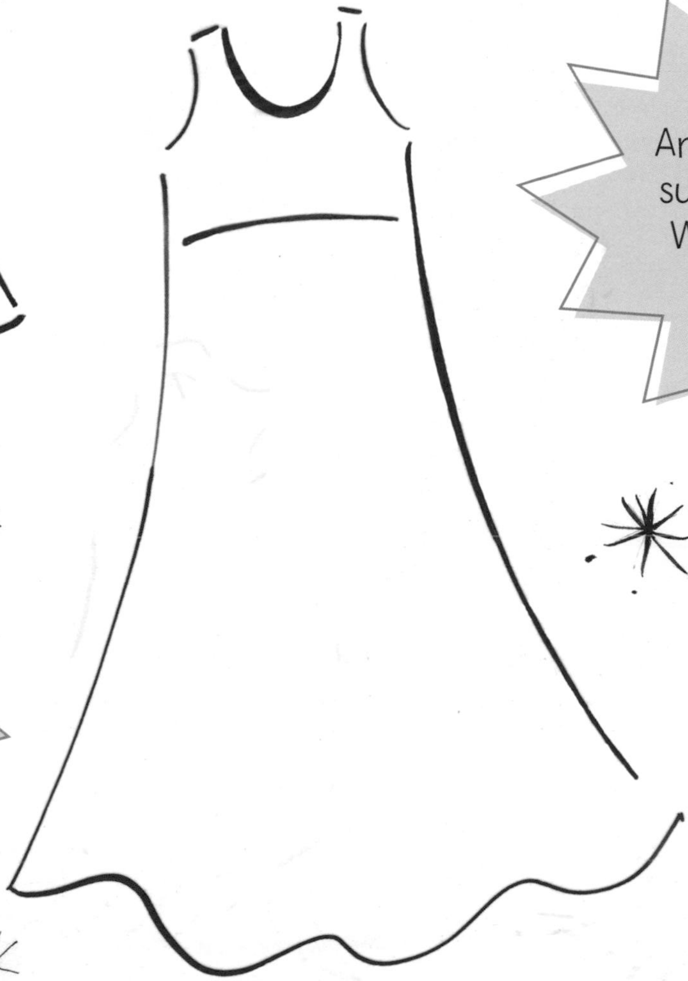

Anna loves floaty summer dresses. What patterns will you choose?

Design a logo for her T-shirt!

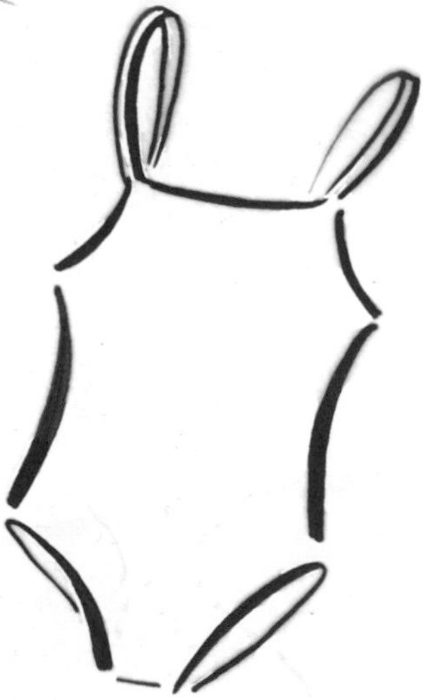

Fill it in!

What's YOUR swimsuit style?

....

Swimathon!

Can you win the swimming race?
Get some friends, get on your marks, and GO!
And don't forget to do the actions...

How to play

For two or more players
Place counters, such as charms or small coins, on the start. Take turns to pick a number from the number chooser. Move your counter along the squares, according to the number you picked.

Follow any instructions you land on. The first to the end is the winner!

Start

Oops, a false start!
Go back to the beginning.

Pretend to do front crawl and move forward 1 space.

You forgot to put on your goggles.
Miss a go.

You hear the crowd cheering.
Go forward 1 space.

Pretend to do the backstroke and move forward 1 space.

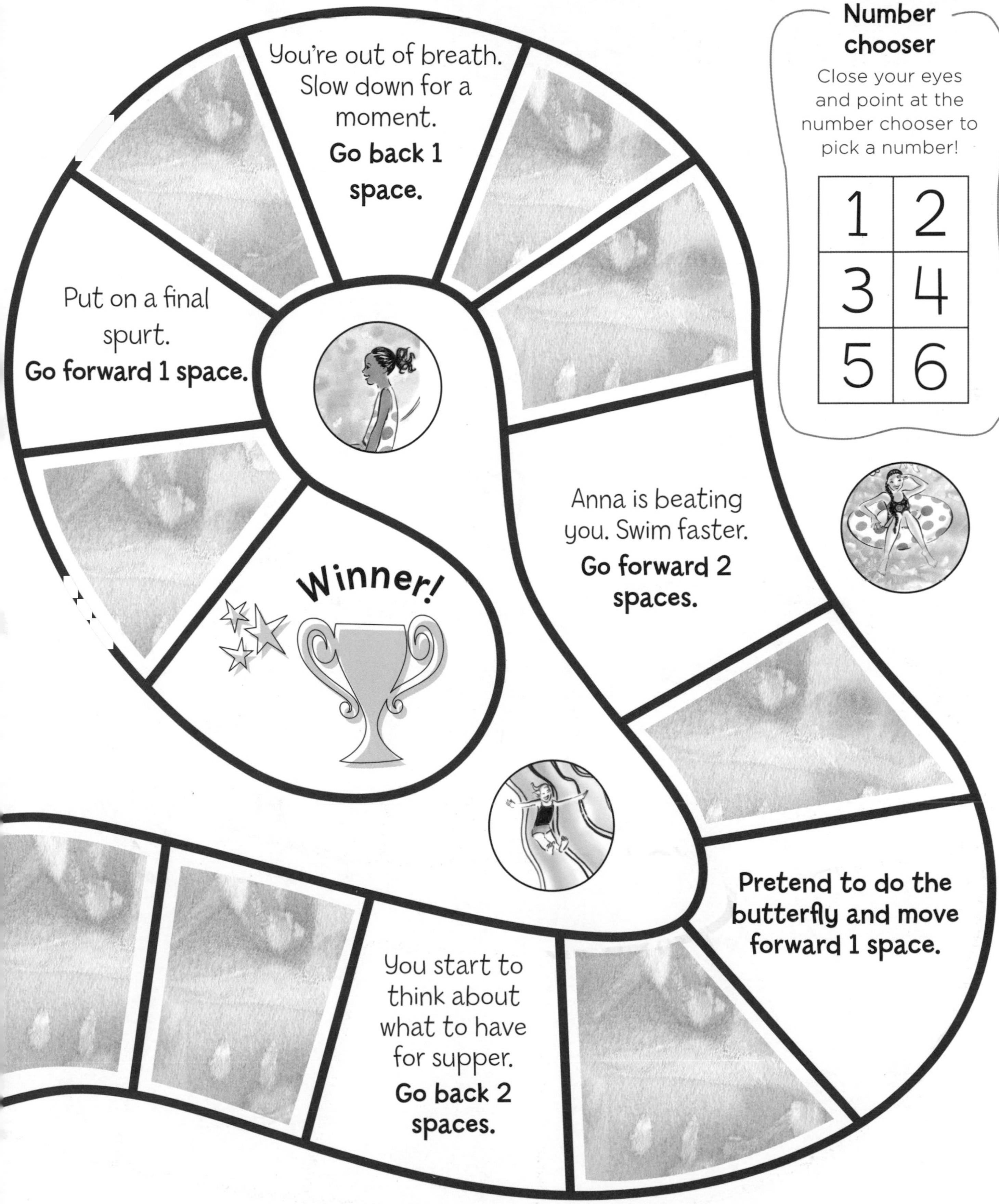
You're out of breath. Slow down for a moment.
Go back 1 space.
Put on a final spurt.
Go forward 1 space.
Winner!
Anna is beating you. Swim faster.
Go forward 2 spaces.
Pretend to do the butterfly and move forward 1 space.
You start to think about what to have for supper.
Go back 2 spaces.

Number chooser

Close your eyes and point at the number chooser to pick a number!

1	2
3	4
5	6

Pretty pool

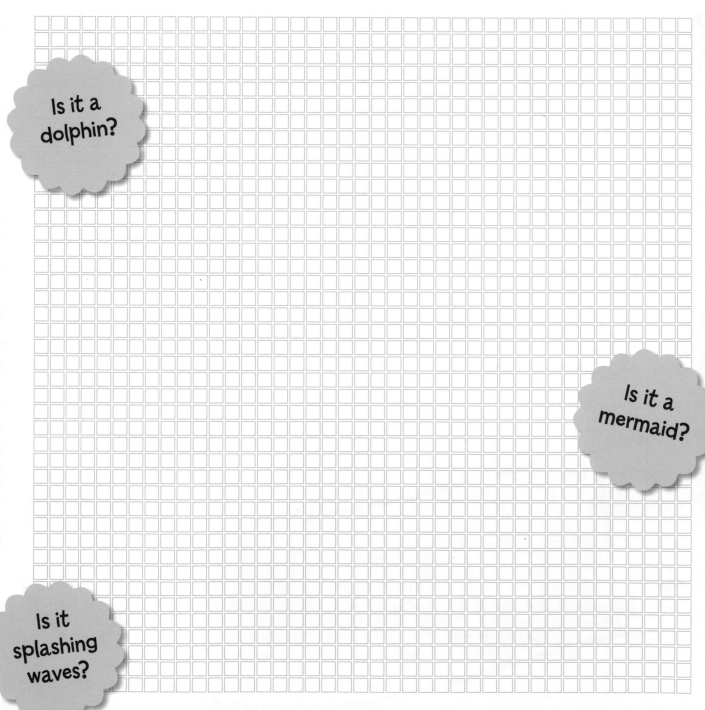

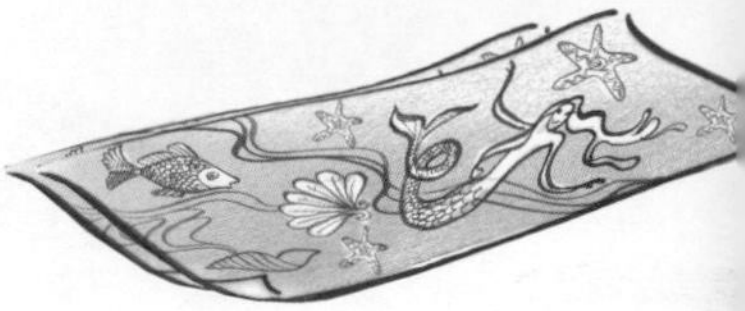

Swimming pools are often covered with pretty mosaic tiles. Each tiny tile is decorated so that they all come together to make a picture. Make your own mosaic here!

Is it a dolphin?

Is it a mermaid?

Is it splashing waves?

Anna's diary

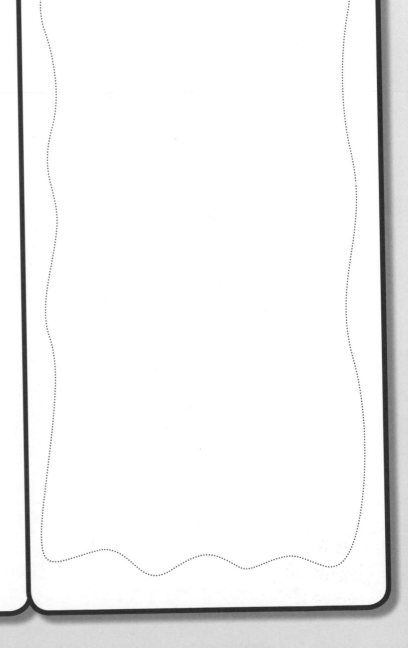

Read Anna's diary page and then draw a picture in the space to match something that she has written about.

SUNDAY

Dear Diary,

We spent the first day of our trip at the water park by the lake. I was so glad that I suggested it because all the girls loved it!

We played in the pool with the water jets and waterfalls. Then we went in the whirlpool and finally rode down the big water slide. We had a picnic lunch with sandwiches and lovely, juicy tomatoes, followed by chocolate cake. Then after a rest, we did it all over again. It was awesome!

Puzzle parade

How many girls' names can you think of beginning with the letter A? Write them here!

Anna

Jess, Anna and Carla entered a swimming competition. In each race, they got 3 points for winning, 2 points for coming in second and 1 point for coming in third and no points for coming in 4th. Who got the most points?

FREESTYLE
Anna: 1st place
Jess: 3rd place
Carla: 4th place

BACKSTROKE
Anna: 3rd place
Jess: 2nd place
Carla: 1st place

BUTTERFLY
Anna: 2nd place
Jess: 3rd place
Carla: 4th place

MEDLEY
Anna: 2nd place
Jess: 1st place
Carla: 3rd place

Write the answer here:

Anna

Twenty questions

Anna and Jess love all kinds of sporty activities.
Join in their quick sporty quiz!

1. Softball is a lot like baseball.
☐ TRUE ✓ FALSE ✗

2. Extreme sports are never dangerous.
☐ TRUE ✓ FALSE ✗

3. Serena Williams is a tennis champion.
☐ TRUE ✓ FALSE ✗

4. The skeleton is a winter sport.
✓ TRUE ☐ FALSE ✓

5. Dancing is an Olympic sport.
☐ TRUE ✓ FALSE ✓

6. Women have never competed in professional boxing.
☐ TRUE ✓ FALSE ✓

7. You use a ball in ice hockey.
☐ TRUE ✓ FALSE ✓

8. The most-played sport in the world is soccer.
✓ TRUE ☐ FALSE ✓

9. In show jumping, men and women compete together.
✓ TRUE ☐ FALSE ✓

10. A martial art is one in which married couples compete.
☐ TRUE ✓ FALSE ✓

11. The ancient Mayans played a ball game a bit like basketball.
✓ TRUE ☐ FALSE ✓

12. BMX riding began in 2005.
☐ TRUE ✓ FALSE ✓

13. Badminton is played with a shuttlestick.
✓ TRUE ✓ FALSE ✗

14. A straddle is a move in trampolining.
✓ TRUE ☐ FALSE ✓

15. Snowboarding is not a competitive sport.
☐ TRUE ✓ FALSE ✓

16. A kind of soccer was played in Europe over 500 years ago.
✓ TRUE ☐ FALSE ✓

17. Dressage is a sport you do on horseback.
☐ TRUE ✓ FALSE ✗

18. An nosegrab is a skateboarding move.
✓ TRUE ☐ FALSE ✓

19. Michael Phelps is a famous golfer.
✓ TRUE ☐ FALSE ✓

20. The Olympics are held once every 10 years.
☐ TRUE ✓ FALSE ✓

Check the answers at the back of the book to find out how many you got right!

Splash out with paint!

Feeling crafty? Here's how to make a great swimming pool scene. It's so easy!

You will need

* White candle or white wax crayon
* Pieces of white paper
* Blue water-based paint
* Paintbrush
* Scissors
* Pens, pencils or crayons
* Craft glue

1 Using the candle or wax crayon, draw shapes to make waves and splashes on a piece of white paper.

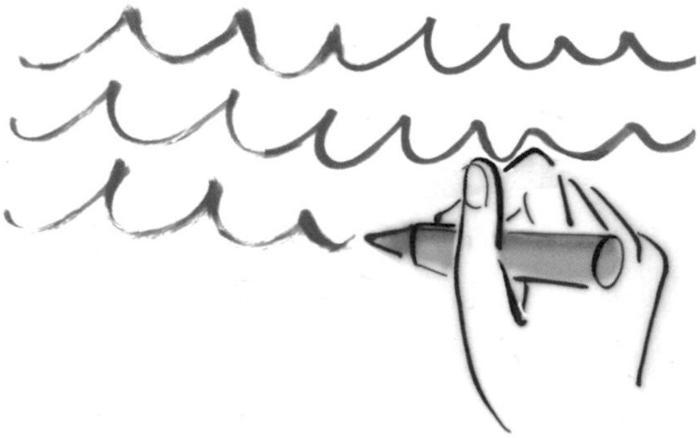

2 Take the blue paint and add lots of water to make a thin "wash".

3 Paint the wash all over the paper and leave it to dry. The shapes you drew with the wax won't hold the paint and will show up as white.

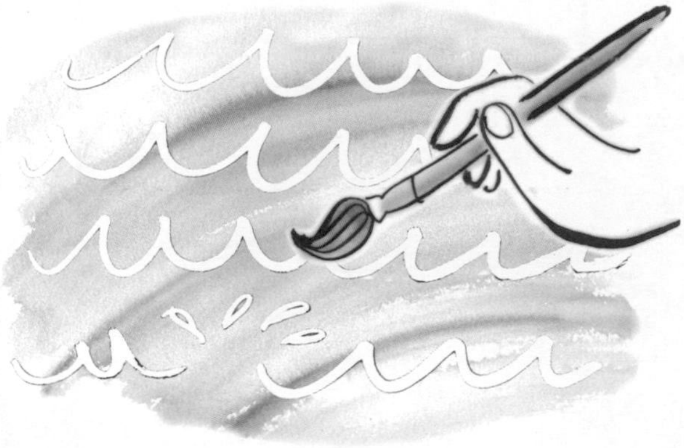

4 Draw swimmers, balls or fish on a piece of paper. Decorate them and then cut them out. Stick them on your pool background.

Now your swimming pool scene is ready to display!

Puzzle parade

Anna wants to swim to the seal float.
Which line leads her to it?

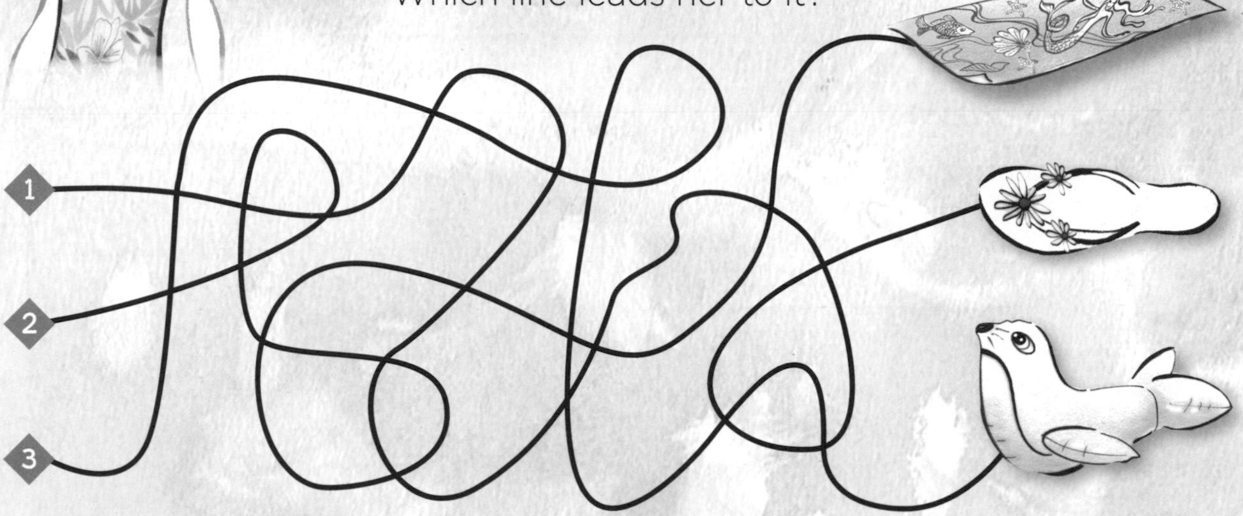

If the number in each beachball is the sum of the two below it, how quickly can you fill in the blanks to solve this puzzle? Go!

Rearrange all the letters in this grid to find some things that the girls definitely need at the pool!

I	T	S
U	S	M
W	I	S

Write the answer here:

....

TOP 10 TIPS for swimming fun!

Follow these tips to make sure you have fun, and stay safe, in the pool!

1. Take lessons

If you can't swim already, try to get lessons. Ask your parents or perhaps you can learn at school. Not only is swimming great fun, it's also good exercise and knowing how to swim keeps you safe around water.

2. Going under...

Get used to putting your head under the water. Take a breath, then duck down and wave to your friends! Some people might find it easier to wear goggles. DON'T breathe in while you're down there!

3. Ring toss

Get used to going underwater by playing a game of ring toss. Ask your swimming teacher or a friend to throw rubber rings around the pool, then duck down and get them.

4. Floating fun!

Good swimmers are good floaters! Do this by putting your head back in the water and pushing your belly button up. When you get the hang of it, it's very relaxing!

5. Different strokes

The first stroke you learn will probably be front crawl. But when you get confident, you can move on to backstroke, breaststroke, and even butterfly!

6. Treading water

This is an important safety skill. Make small rotating moves with your hands (sculling) and paddle with your legs to stay upright in the water. Do this if you accidentally get out of your depth and need to rest.

7. Diving diva

Why not ask your swimming teacher if you can learn how to dive, too? Remember, only dive where you're allowed to do so and NEVER dive in shallow water.

8. Splash out!

Splashing around with friends can be great fun. You can play in the pool with floats and balls. Or how about a game of water piggy-in-the-middle?

9. Go for a gala

If you start to really enjoy swimming, you could join a club at your school or local pool. And if you like competing, you can enter swimming galas and go for gold medals!

10. Last but not least...

Follow the pool rules and always obey instructions from the adults who are in charge. Remember, they are responsible for everyone's safety!

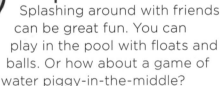

Let's go riding!

Carla loves animals and one of the hobbies she likes best is horse riding. Unscramble the letters below to find something that Carla never goes anywhere without.

Find it!

Carla's riding hat is hiding somewhere in this chapter. It looks like this...

TOHOP FO ERH REHSO

Write the answer here:

....

PART 3

Continued from page 26...

Taylor's trip

It's Carla's turn to organize the day's activities and she has even planned a little surprise for Taylor!

Carla mounted her horse, landing lightly in the saddle. She gathered the reins and looked round to see how her friends were getting on. It was the third day of the stay at Lake Truly and Carla had brought them to the nearby Lakeside Riding Stables.

Now, she cast her eye over her friends and was pleased to see most of them up in the saddle. But there was a small problem: Taylor was standing in the middle of the yard with no horse!

"Let's go!" called Jess eagerly, not seeing that poor Taylor was stranded.

"I can't!" Taylor replied. "I don't have a horse!"

"I definitely booked six horses," Carla replied. "Where's the stable girl gone?" Carla looked around and frowned. She had been clear about what she wanted when she booked.

"This is typical," Taylor said dramatically, flinging her arms out. "I can't have dance lessons and now I can't go riding either!"

The girls looked at each other in dismay. Anna whispered to Jess,

"We can't leave Taylor behind, she's the one we're cheering up!"

Just then, the stable girl reappeared leading one of the prettiest horses that Carla had EVER seen. She was deep chestnut, with a long, silky mane. But her most striking feature was an almost perfect white star on her forehead.

"Sorry for the slight delay," the girl said. "This is Stella. It means 'star.'"

"She's beautiful!" said Taylor.

Carla grinned. Her plans had worked out after all. "And she's all yours for the whole morning!" she said to Taylor.

"Me?" Taylor was now smiling from ear to ear. "Wow!"

"Well," Carla explained with a giggle, "I thought you and Stella would make a good match as she's the 'star' of the show just like you!"

Taylor grinned and patted Stella's neck.

"Great," said Jess. "NOW let's go!" she cried as everybody happily headed off for their ride.

Continued on page 74...

Horsey doodle!

What kind of riding hat would you like to wear?
Doodle one for you and one for your best friend!

Does it have a cool pattern?

Does it have a logo?

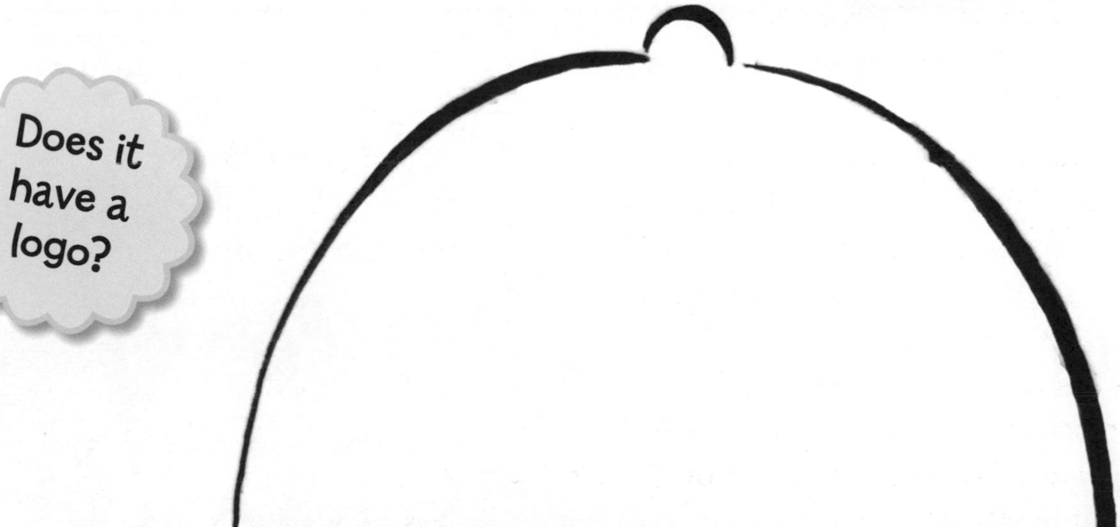

Spot the difference

There are ten tricky differences between these two pictures of the girls riding. Ring them when you've found them!

A

B

What's your sport?

Answer the questions and follow the arrows to find out which sport suits YOU!

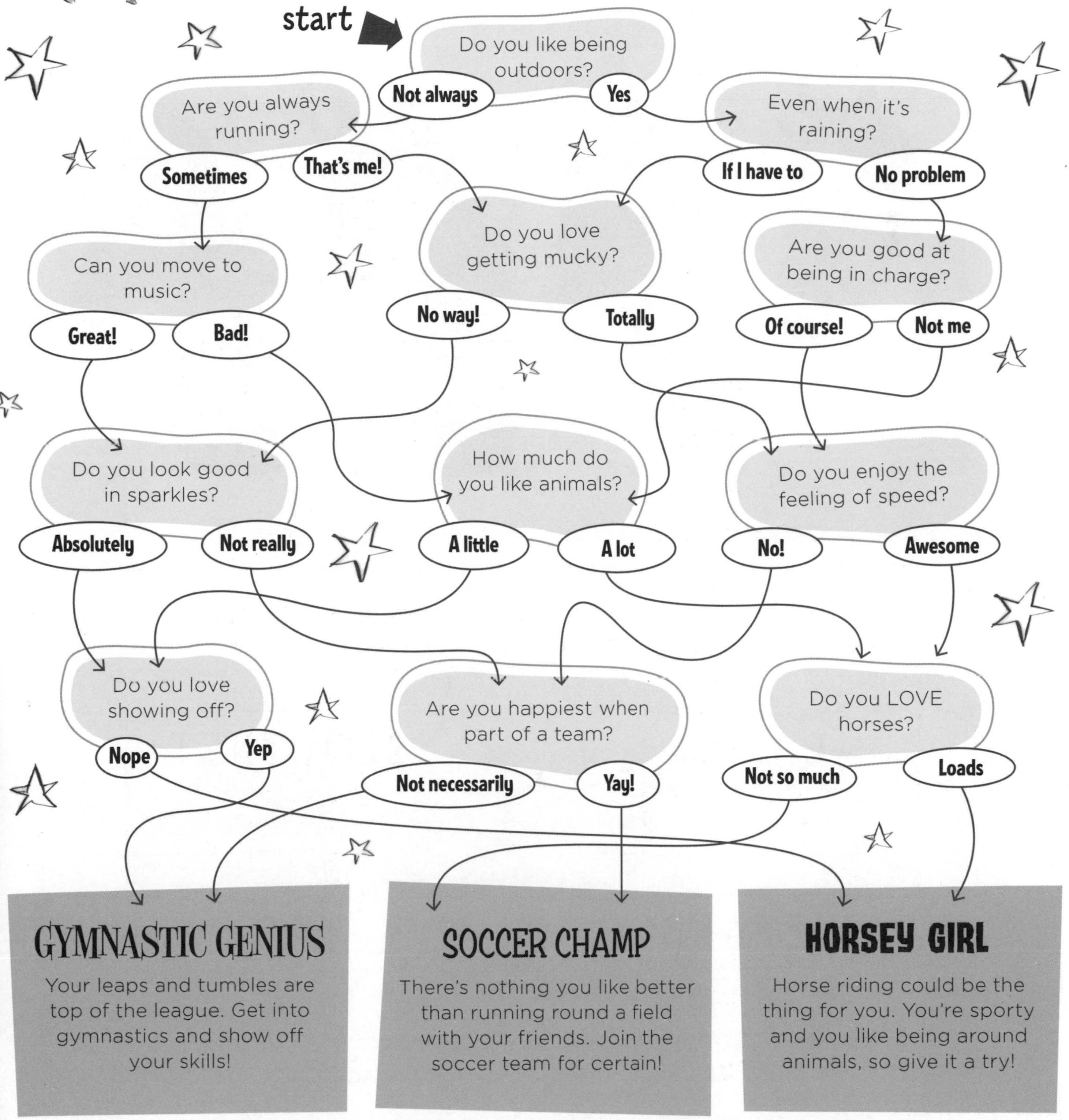

GYMNASTIC GENIUS

Your leaps and tumbles are top of the league. Get into gymnastics and show off your skills!

SOCCER CHAMP

There's nothing you like better than running round a field with your friends. Join the soccer team for certain!

HORSEY GIRL

Horse riding could be the thing for you. You're sporty and you like being around animals, so give it a try!

Puzzle parade

Which shadow exactly matches the horse's head?

Unscramble the letters in each word to find four common names for horses' coats.

CABKL ....

SHUCTNET ....

DIEPALB ....

YAB ....

Chase the horse!

One naughty horse doesn't want to be caught.
Help Carla chase after him across the field!

start

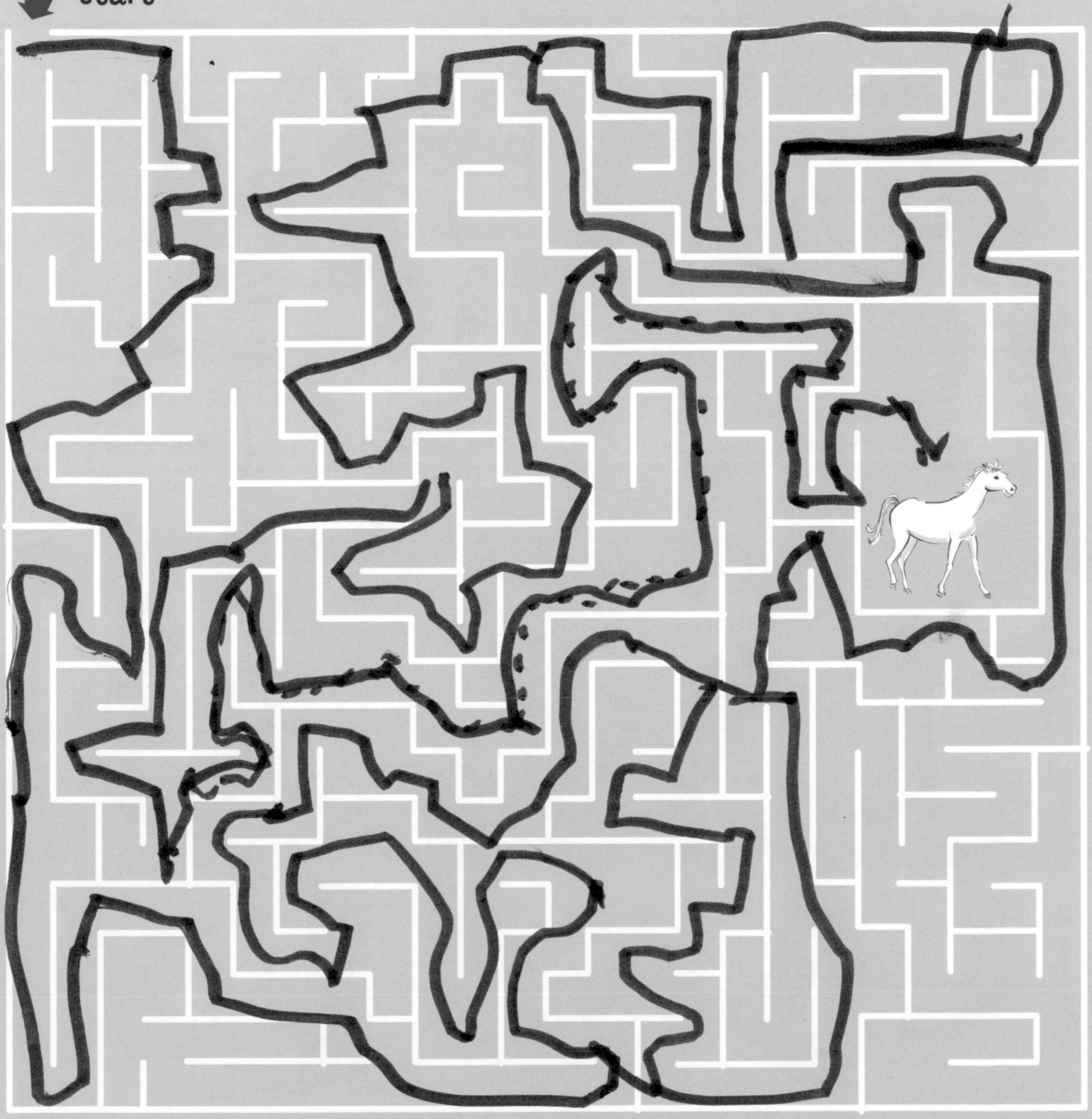

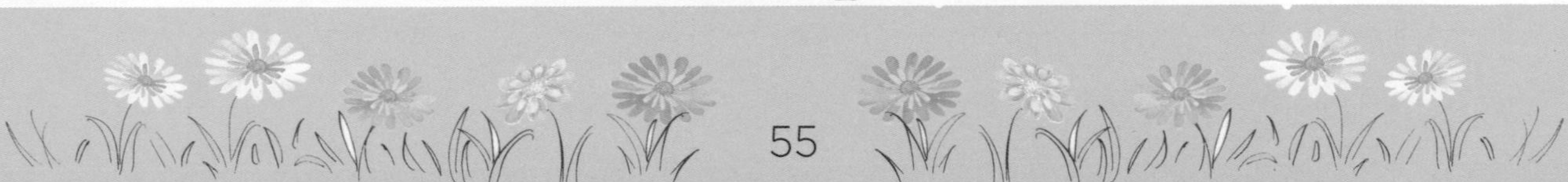

Puzzle parade

Carla is getting ready to ride. Take her around the maze to pick up first her hat and then her boots. Can you do it without going back on yourself?

The girls borrow riding boots from the stables but they are all in a jumble. Can you find the boot with no pair?

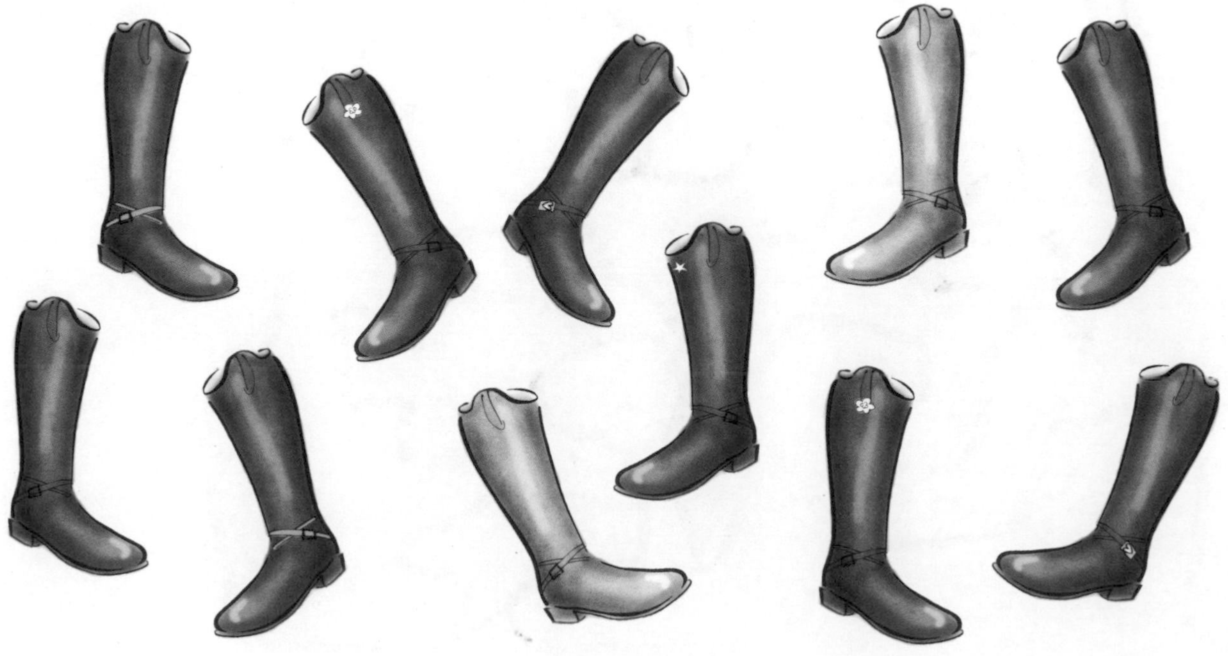

Draw Carla!

Copy Carla's picture into the grid square by square.

CARLA'S FASHION TIP
Use a cute scarf as a hairband to keep your hair tidy!

Fill it in!

What's YOUR best hair accessory?

....

....

Message me!

Carla has received a text message from her sister Sadie. Begin at the shaded square and trace a path through the letters to spell out the message. Go up, down, forward or backward but not diagonally.

S	I	H	O	S	K	E	B	H	O	S	E
L	H	K	V	E	A	M	D	L	U	R	H
Y	O	R	A	N	L	R	U	L	N	P	F
O	P	Y	D	S	L	E	Y	O	O	H	P
N	E	Y	O	U	K	P	I	M	E	J	N
B	A	K	I	A	T	I	M	E	O	N	T
C	L	A	B	R	T	A	E	R	G	A	H
U	S	K	I	E	H	A	V	I	N	G	E
S	S	I	O	L	N	O	R	E	Y	I	T
A	D	N	O	S	D	F	E	M	O	L	R
D	Z	A	D	M	S	A	A	I	U	O	I
H	S	R	S	C	A	N	M	T	R	H	P

end

Write the message here:

Which is which?

Carla is at the stables and working out which of her friends can ride which horse and what each horse looks like. Use the six clues to fill in the rows and columns and discover Carla's plan.

Clues

1. Taylor's horse is the chestnut. Her name is Stella.
2. Anna's horse is not black or piebald.
3. Milly's horse is not called Jensen.
4. Jess's horse is called Duke. He isn't palomino.
5. Jolly is being ridden by Roxy and isn't black.
6. The girl who is riding the bay horse knows her horse is called Rocket.

HINT
If you know an answer, cross out the other boxes along the row and column.

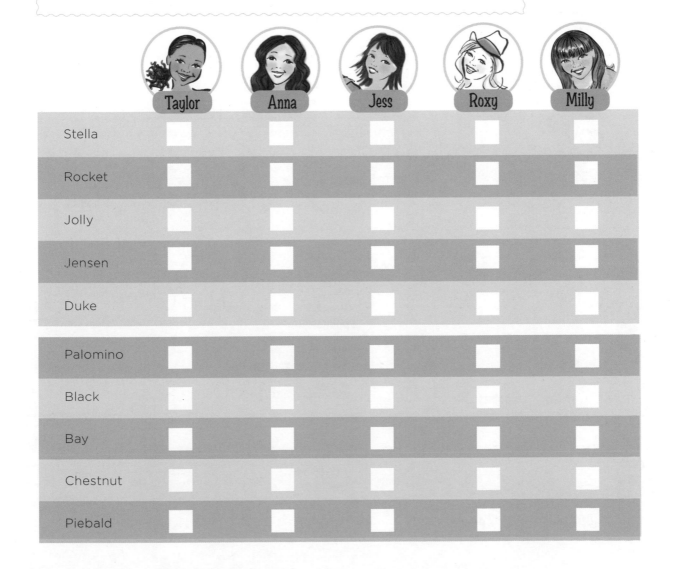

	Taylor	Anna	Jess	Roxy	Milly
Stella					
Rocket					
Jolly					
Jensen					
Duke					
Palomino					
Black					
Bay					
Chestnut					
Piebald					

Ready, steady, gallop!

Carla has entered a riding competition with five rounds. How quickly can you add up her points in each round? Try and do it in your head without writing anything down!

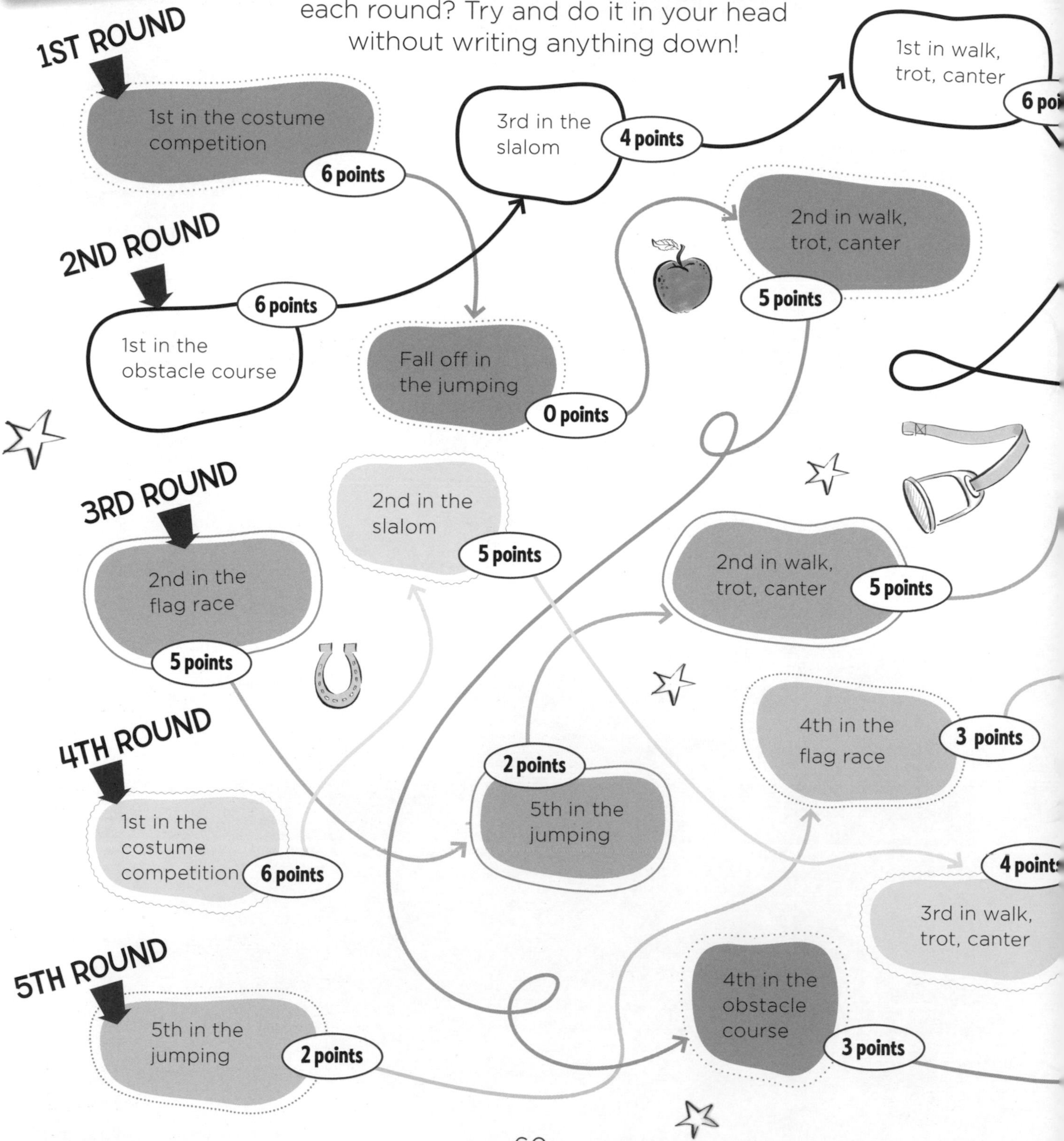

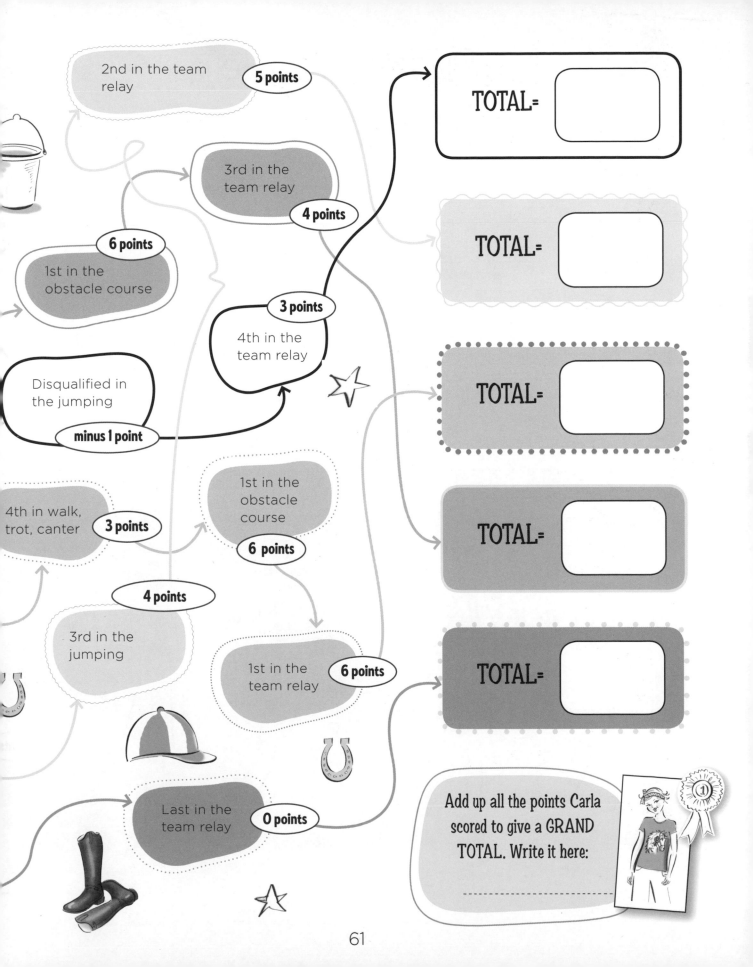

2nd in the team relay — 5 points

3rd in the team relay — 4 points

1st in the obstacle course — 6 points

4th in the team relay — 3 points

Disqualified in the jumping — minus 1 point

4th in walk, trot, canter — 3 points

1st in the obstacle course — 6 points

3rd in the jumping — 4 points

1st in the team relay — 6 points

Last in the team relay — 0 points

TOTAL=

TOTAL=

TOTAL=

TOTAL=

TOTAL=

Add up all the points Carla scored to give a GRAND TOTAL. Write it here:

Puzzle parade

Help Carla pick up all the buckets and horseshoes in the stable yard.

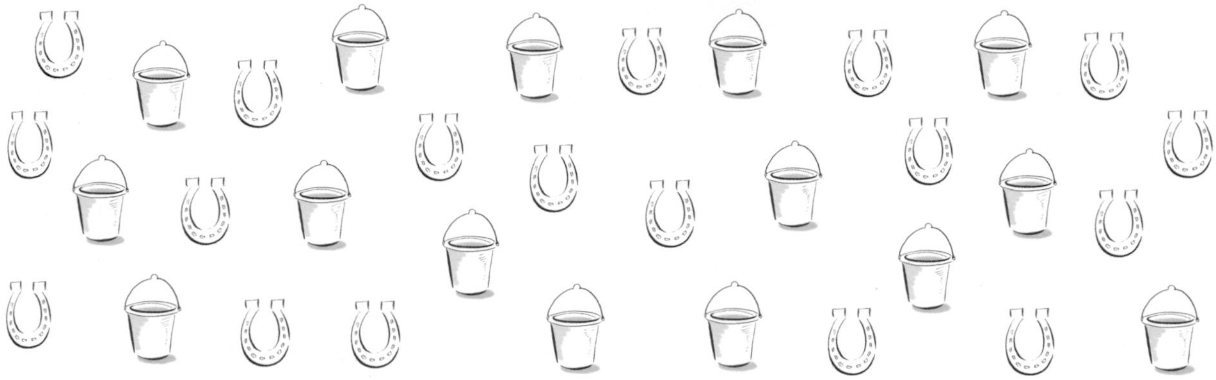

How many buckets? .... How many horseshoes? ....

Which picture of Carla is the odd one out?

Carla's top fashion

Add pretty shades and patterns to make an outfit for Carla to wear on her trip.

Add buttons to her cardigan!

Shade in Carla's cute shoes to match her outfit!

Pick a pattern for her dress!

Fill it in!

What funky shoes would YOU pick to go with your best outfit?

....

Super spot the difference!

Are you eagle-eyed? There are twelve VERY tricky differences between these two pictures of Taylor, Carla and Anna. Can you find them all? Good luck!

How many did you spot?

Shade in a shape each time you find a difference!

Over the stable door...

Who's looking over the stable door?
Doodle your perfect pony and write his name above the door.

What's his coat like?
Is his mane braided?
Does he have any markings?

Carla's diary

Fill in the blanks in Carla's diary with words from the panel. Choose carefully!

Dear Diary,

You never guess what my .... did today! She .... and then she .... right after. I had to stop myself .... Anyway, it all ended OK and later in the afternoon we went to the .... and .... I'm glad Taylor invited us on on this trip. When I get home I'm going to give her ....

fair

having hysterics

ocolate

horse

ugged me

Anna

riding lessons

ate pizza

galloped away

relaxed

snorted

laughing

flowers

café

Puzzle parade

How many words can you make from the letters in RIDING STABLES?

Help Carla find her horse's feeding bucket. It's the one with two stars on the side!

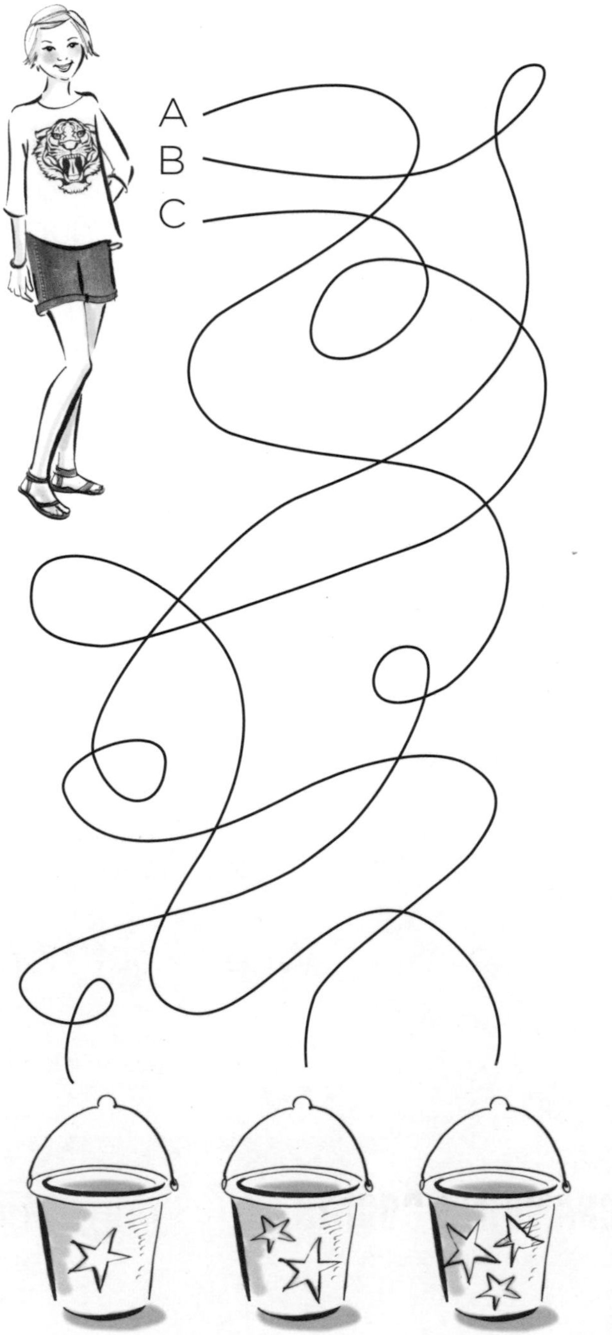

Two's company!

You're at a hotel and you're sharing a room. Do this quiz with your best friend, answering yes or no to each question. Add up how many you got the same and find out if you're born to be roomies!

	YOU	YOUR BEST FRIEND
1 Do you wake up mega-early every morning?		
2 Do you put your clothes away neatly?		
3 Do you leave your books and mags lying around?		
4 Do you snore in your sleep?		
5 Do you like to read in bed before you turn the light out?		
6 Do you like the room to be cool so you can sleep?		
7 Do you hog the bathroom every morning?		
8 Do you take forever to decide what to wear?		
9 Do you put the radio on?		
10 Do you like to decorate the room with all your knick-knacks?		

1 - 3

CHANGING ROOMS

You might be best friends but you'll run into trouble sharing a room. Swap with someone else!

4 - 7

ROOM FOR IMPROVEMENT

If you can put up with your best friend's little habits, a room-share could work out nicely!

8 - 10

ROOM MATES

Yay! You two are born to be together. Sharing a room will be loads of fun!

Horseshoe photo frame

Horseshoes are supposed to bring good luck. Here's how to make a lucky horseshoe photo frame to show off a happy souvenir photo!

You will need

* Silver cardboard
* Pencil
* Scissors
* Photo for frame
* Craft glue
* String or ribbon

1. Using the template here, draw a horseshoe shape on the silver cardboard. Cut it out.
2. Ask an adult to help you poke holes through where the circles are.
3. Choose a photo that is slightly bigger than your horseshoe shape. Lay it down face up and put the horseshoe on top. Line up the top of the photo with the top of the horseshoe.
4. Draw round the inner edge of the horseshoe in pencil. Cut out the photo around the outside of the pencil mark, leaving about 0.5 inches (1 cm) around the outside edge.
5. Use glue to stick the photo to the back of the horseshoe. Let it dry, then thread rustic-looking string or thin rope through the top two holes and knot securely to hang it up!

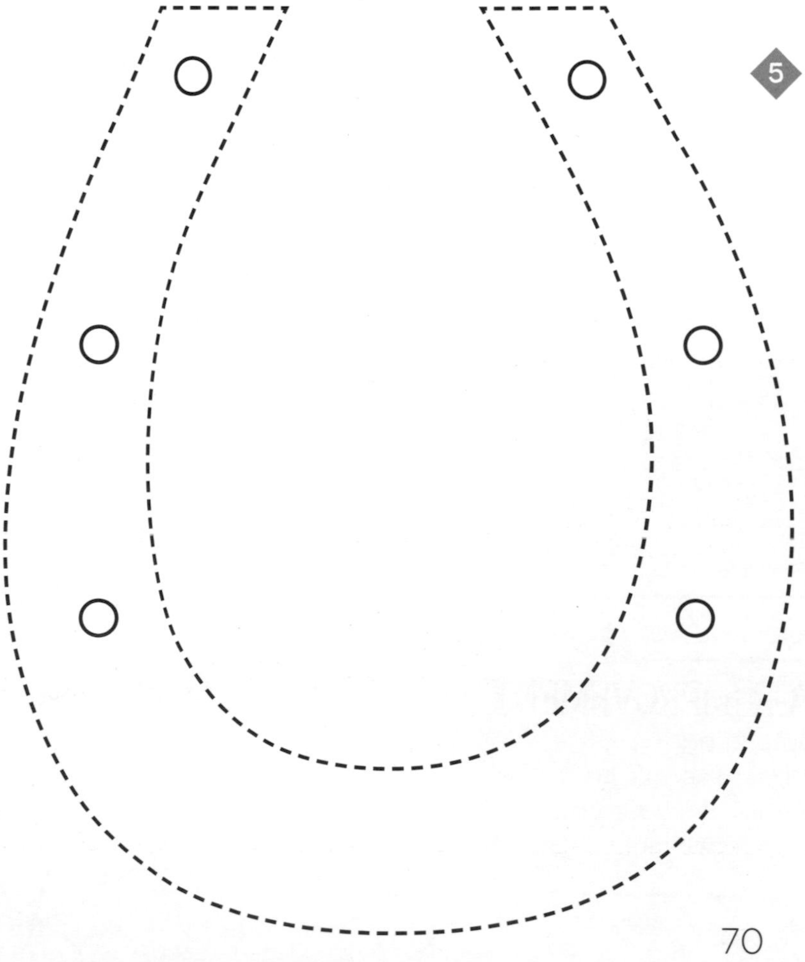

Puzzle parade

Look at Taylor riding her horse. Can you spot five differences between picture 1 and picture 2?

Unscramble the names of the horses at the Lakeside Riding Stables. Look back at page 59 if you need help!

YOLLJ ....

CEKROT ....

TELSAL ....

KEDU ....

NESNEJ ....

10 TOP TIPS..... for starting riding

Ever felt like learning to ride but never tried it? Here are ten top tips to help you get started...

1. Find a school

Unless you're lucky enough to know someone with a pony who can give you lessons, the only way to learn is at a riding school. They can be expensive, so take a look around your local area to find a good one that you can afford.

2. Hard hat

You need a riding hat for safety. You may fall off, especially when you are learning, so you need to protect your head. The riding school may lend you one at first, but it's best to get your own eventually.

3. Get the gear

The full riding gear will cost you lots of money, but you don't need it all at once. But you do need a pair of jodhpurs and boots for comfort and to help you sit properly on the horse. Look for secondhand ones if you're on a budget.

4. Confidence counts

As with many sports, you need lots of confidence. It feels strange to sit so high up on a pony or horse the first few times you do it, so pluck up your courage!

5. Take control

You have to learn to be in control of the pony, not the other way round. So don't forget, you're in charge! Be firm and make sure he does what you want.

6. The basics: hands

Your teacher will take you through the basics, but there are some important points to remember. The first is the position of your hands. Hold the reins lightly but firmly so that you have gentle contact with the horse's mouth.

7. The basics: seat

The way you sit is very important, too. Sit upright in the middle of the saddle with your back straight and your shoulders back. And don't forget to relax!

8. The basics: legs

Adjust your stirrups so that your legs are in the right position, with knees slightly bent. Rest the balls of your feet on the strirrups and keep your heels down.

9. Through the paces

Over a course of lessons, you will learn the basics of how to communicate with the pony. You will find out how to take him through his paces: walking, trotting and cantering. You can even learn how to jump. When you get good, you can compete in gymkhanas and win rosettes and prizes!

10. Saddle up!

If you save enough cash, you can go on horseriding weekends or even longer trips. There are lots to choose from, but be prepared for long days in the saddle. Ouch!

Fun at the fair!

Milly's idea of fun is to spend the day at the fair. Unscramble the letters below to find something that she's going to buy!

TOH GDO TIWH CEKPHUT

Write the answer here:

....

....

Find it!

Milly's sun hat is hiding somewhere in this chapter. It looks like this...

Taylor's trip

PART 4
Continued from page 50...

The girls laze around on the lawn outside their cabin and chat about what to do today. It's Milly's turn to decide!

"Did anybody see the poster at the stables yesterday?" Milly asked. The girls were listening eagerly. "A fair is opening at Lake Truly today. We should go!"

"Fantastic, we're going!" said Anna.

That afternoon, the girls found the fair buzzing with people.

"Let's go on the Ferris wheel," suggested Milly.

"Great idea," said Jess, while Carla and Anna nodded in agreement.

"Roxy and I want to get a drink first," said Taylor. "We'll meet you back here."

"OK," Milly replied. "Let's go!"

The Ferris wheel was amazing. The friends had an incredible view of the fairground and Lake Truly in the distance. The people below looked like scurrying ants and the girls spotted a ghost train, a pirate ship and a merry-go-round. There was so much to do!

"Look," shouted Anna. "Isn't that Taylor? What IS she doing?" Anna pointed down below to a booth where Taylor was flinging her arms around.

"Oh no," Milly cried. "She looks a bit cross."

"There's Roxy, too," Jess added. "She's doing the same. She's waving her arms in Taylor's face. They're having an argument!"

"We'd better get over there, quick!" Carla said.

As soon as the ride finished, the four girls dashed over to the booth. As they got closer, they heard music pumping and Taylor was yelling. They ran into the booth, just as Roxy was pointing right at Taylor.

"Roxy! Taylor! Stop arguing!" Milly shouted anxiously above the noise.

The two girls stopped in surprise.

"We're not arguing," Taylor laughed. It's a dance competition. We have to copy the moves on the screen."

"Watch me!" Roxy grinned and they both started leaping about again.

The others burst out laughing.

"I guess we'd better join in," Jess said. And then the dance competition really began!

Continued on page 98...

Bunch of balloons

Milly and the girls buy some balloons at the fair.
Doodle on them!

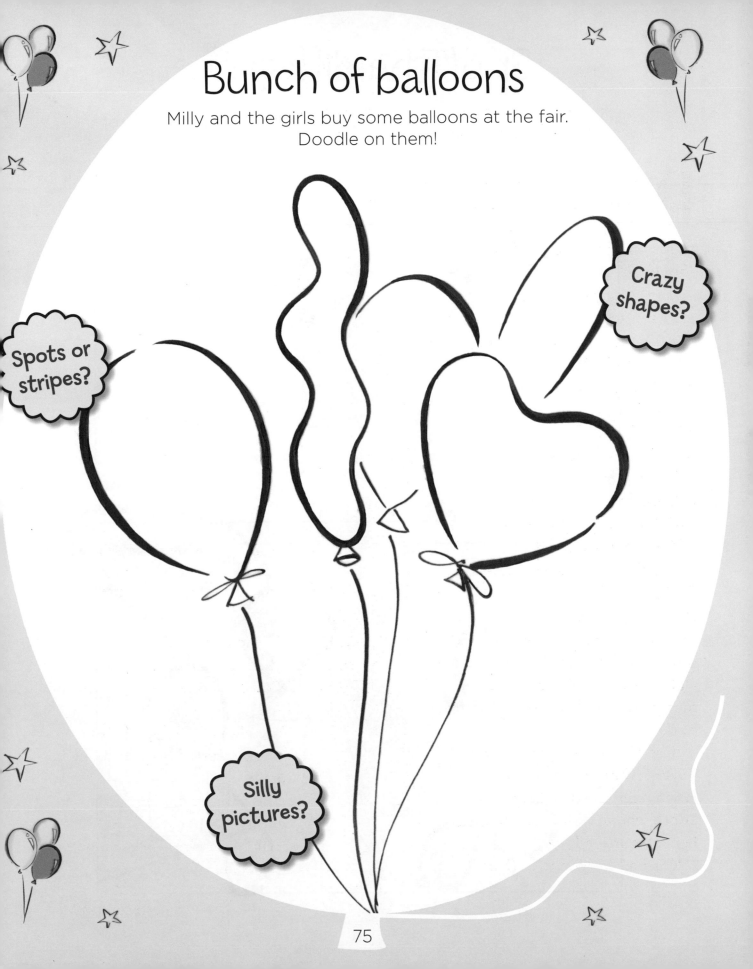

Spot the difference

There are ten tricky differences between these two pictures of the girls at the fair. Ring them when you've found them!

A

B

What's your fairground fun?

Read the questions and circle your answers. Did you get mostly As, Bs or Cs? Check the panel to find out which fairground attraction you make a beeline for!

1 What would be your best birthday present?

A. a collection of computer games

B. a skateboard

C. lunch at a fancy pizza restaurant with all your friends

2 If you joined a new club at school, what would it be?

A. chess club

B. rock climbing club

C. art and crafts club

3 In a bookstore, what would you rather buy?

A. a puzzle book

B. an adventure story

C. a recipe book

4 How would you like to spend a sunny day?

A. at a tennis tournament

B. on a cycle ride

C. at a picnic

5 A friend is coming to visit. What do you do?

A. challenge her to a game of badminton

B. take her to the latest big action movie

C. plan to spend the afternoon making cookies

MOSTLY As

GAMES GALORE

You love competition so hang out in the games arcade and stay until you win something!

MOSTLY Bs

THRILLS AND SPILLS

You're a thrill seeker and you love the feeling of speed. Get on that rollercoaster and scream!

MOSTLY Cs

FOOD FAN

You just can't resist the delicious food stalls. Go straight for the hot dogs, then finish with a toffee apple!

Puzzle parade

Which picture of the merry-go-round is the odd one out?

1

2

3

Unscramble these letters to find a fairground ride!

EFRISR LEWHE

Write the answer here

Shade in the balloons so that every row, column and square contains one red, one blue, one green and one yellow.

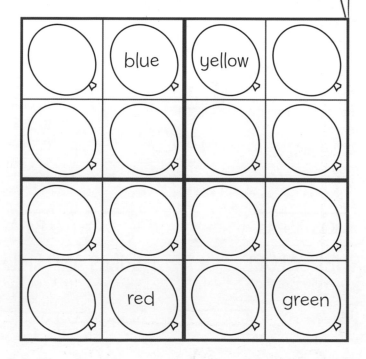

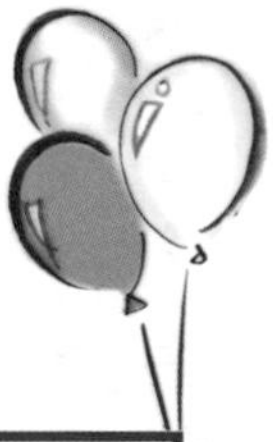

	blue	yellow	
	red		green

Mirror maze

Milly makes her way inside the mirror maze, so help her find her way out. She must pass all the mirrors before she gets to the exit.

Puzzle parade

Which shadow matches the picture of Milly?

Milly needs 25 credits to play the dance game in the arcade.
Which three tokens can she use?

Draw Milly!

Copy Milly's picture into the grid, square by square.

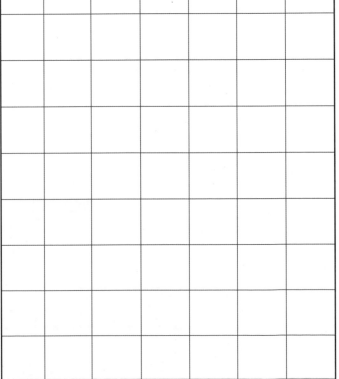

MILLY'S FASHION TIP
Always wear a hat in the sun. It protects your head and it looks SO cute!

Fill it in!

What would YOU wear on a hot day?

....

....

Milly's secret message

From Milly's coded message, can you work out where the girls are going next at the fairground and what their secret is? Read opposite to find out how!

22 19 | 10 15 19 | 20 21 3 13 20

6 21 | 6 26 19 | 20 26 21 25 6

6 15 10 3 13 | 13 19 8 6. | 1 10 13

17 21 7 | 12 19 19 24 | 10

25 19 1 15 19 6? | 15 21 8 17 | 3 25

2 19 19 14 3 13 20 | 25 1 10 15 19 11!

Each number in the message represents a letter. Begin the puzzle by filling in the letters in the grid below into the secret message.

When you have decoded several letters in a word, you might be able to guess what the missing letters are. When you figure it out, write the letter in the grid below, and then look to see if it is used in any other word. Carry on until the whole message is decoded!

A	B	C	D	E	F	G	H	I	J	K	L	M
				19			26					

N	O	P	Q	R	S	T	U	V	W	X	Y	Z
					25					8		

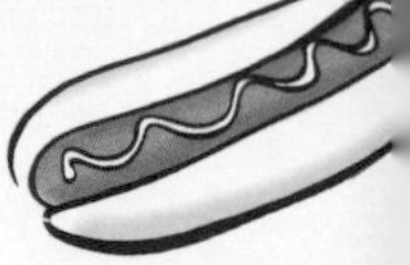

Fairground search

Find the fairground attractions in the grid. Look up, down, backward, across and diagonally.

Word list

arcade
balloons
candycanes
drinks
Ferris wheel
games
ghost train
hot dogs
merry-go-round
prizes
rides
stands

M	N	I	A	R	T	T	S	O	H	G	F
K	E	I	I	S	D	N	A	T	S	R	E
Y	D	R	O	N	L	G	A	M	E	S	R
O	H	M	R	I	D	E	S	A	Z	N	R
N	O	O	T	Y	U	L	Y	R	I	O	I
B	T	N	S	I	G	B	Z	N	R	O	S
C	D	D	K	N	I	O	A	E	P	L	W
U	O	M	N	T	H	R	R	T	L	L	H
J	G	E	I	I	C	D	Q	O	U	A	E
A	S	A	R	A	O	F	A	H	U	B	E
C	A	N	D	Y	C	A	N	E	S	N	L
H	S	E	Q	O	Z	T	R	V	U	Q	D

Where's the show?

The girls want to see the dance show at the fair. In Milly's leaflet, the tent looks exactly like this. Can you find the right one?

1

2

3

4

5

Puzzle parade

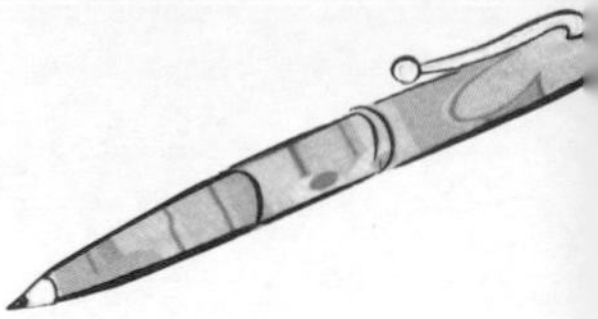

How many girl's names can you think of beginning with the letter M? Write them here!

Milly

Look at these two pictures of Milly's pen and diary. Can you spot five differences between them?

1

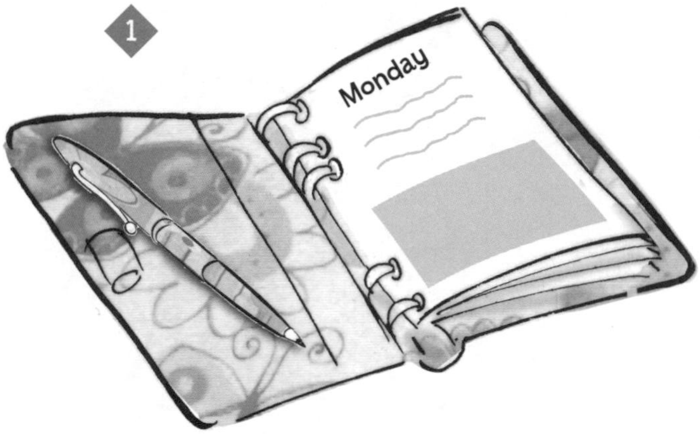

2

Milly's top fashion

Add pretty shades and patterns to make outfits for Milly to wear on her trip.

Design a pattern for her dress!

Do her jogging pants match her top?

What pattern does she have on her ankle boots?

Feast of fun

The girls decide to have a feast to celebrate their fun day at the fair. Milly goes shopping and buys all these items.

Look at the picture for one minute and then close the book. Scribble down on a piece of paper everthing that you can remember! How many did you get right?

Puzzle parade

Fill in the missing letters to spell out words related Milly and her trip to Lake Truly.

PH_TOS

_IRLS

_ABIN

F_OD

FA_R

FRIE_DS

PAR_

Then rearrange the missing letters to find a hobby that Milly loves.

Write the answer here

Which of two of these hot dogs are exactly the same?

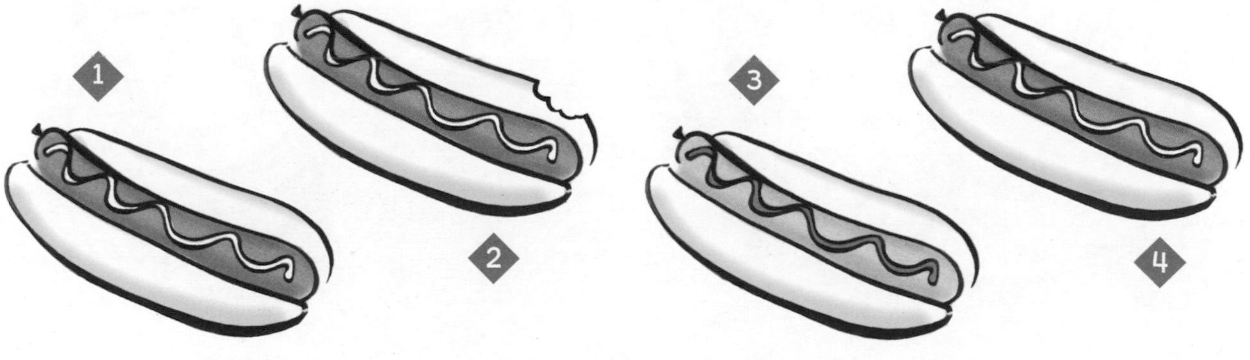

Take a trip!

What if your family can't decide what sort of trip they want to go on? Challenge each member of your family with this questionnaire and then get planning!

QUESTIONNAIRE

1. Do you want to stay:
   a) near home
   b) farther away
   c) in another country

2. Do you want to travel:
   a) by car
   b) by train
   c) by plane

3. Do you want to go to:
   a) a city
   b) the countryside
   c) a beach

4. Do you want to stay in:
   a) a tent
   b) a hotel
   c) a cottage

5. Do you want to:
   a) laze about by the pool
   b) do loads of sporty activities
   c) spend your time sightseeing

6. Your best treat of the whole trip would be:
   a) going out for a delicious meal
   b) going shopping for souvenirs
   c) going to a theme park

7. If you could do one totally amazing thing on your trip, would it be:
   a) swimming with dolphins
   b) visiting an ancient ruin
   c) walking up a mountain

8. And finally, if you already have a travel destination in mind, write it here:

....

Photocopy the questionnaire or just read it out to your family!

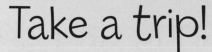

Sunny day dress

Doodle pretty patterns on
Milly's summer dress!

Bright florals?
Summer shades?
Cool patterns?

Fill it in!

What's YOUR
best summer dress?

....

....

Milly's diary

Milly has written four things about the girls' trip to the fair. Can you put them in the right order? Write 1st, 2nd, 3rd or 4th in each box.

Tuesday

When the scary stuff was over, we thought it was time for a break. We found a cool café and ordered milkshakes!

After all our chatting, we decided to go on the ghost train next. Roxy was feeling a little bit scared but we persuaded her that it was going to be fun! Not sure if she agreed...

When we got to the fair, we couldn't wait to go on the Ferris wheel. We had a great view of the fairground and Lake Truly looked so beautiful in the morning sunshine.

The sun was hot at midday so we found a shady spot and ate hot dogs. There was so much left to do at the fair, so we spent ages chatting about what to do next.

Make an ice-cream sundae

Making food for your friends? Then finish off the meal with an ice-cream sundae for dessert. It couldn't be easier!

Try out different ice creams, sauces and fruit toppings!

You will need

* Tall glass or sundae dish
* Serving spoon
* Long ice-cream spoon (if you have one) for eating
* Vanilla ice cream
* Whipped cream
* Strawberry sauce or syrup
* Cherry for decoration

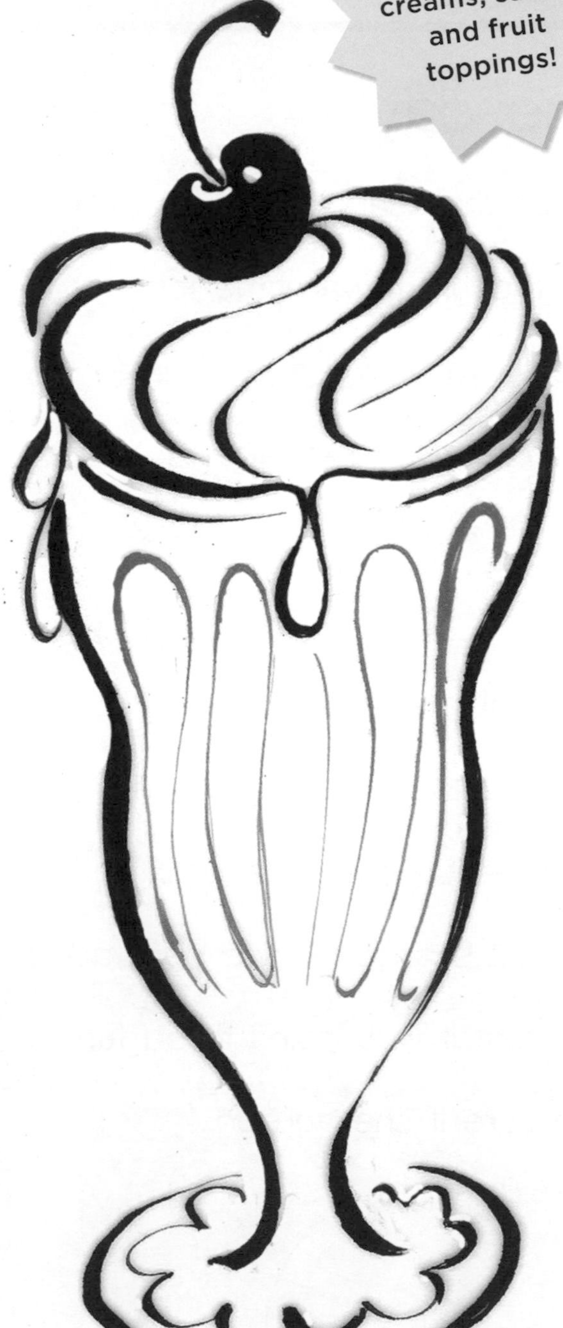

1. Spoon a generous helping of vanilla ice cream into your sundae dish, until it's about three-quarters full.
2. Cover the top of the ice cream with a dollop of whipped cream.
3. Trickle strawberry sauce over the whipped cream in a circular pattern to make a spiral of sauce over the cream.
4. Pop a cherry on the top for decoration. You can use either a fresh cherry or a preserved maraschino cherry from a jar. Your sundae is now ready to enjoy!

Fill it in!

What's YOUR most delicious ice cream?

....

....

Puzzle parade

There are six pictures of Milly here. Can you match up the three pairs?

Oops, Milly has lost her last token for the games arcade.
Which line takes her to it?

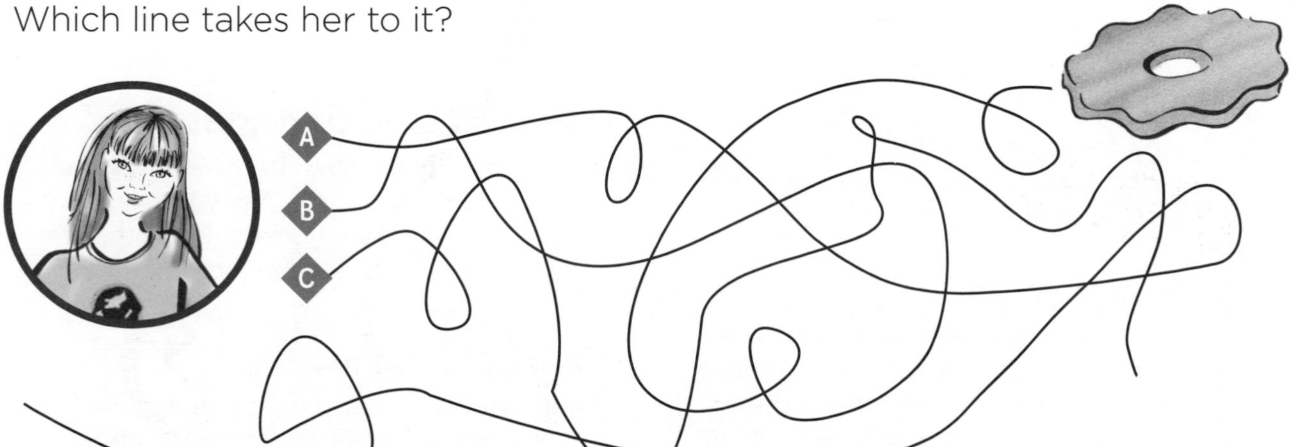

TOP 10 TIPS... to make your own fairground!

Everybody loves a fairground, so why not make your own to entertain your friends? Or you could make it a great theme for a party!

1. The fairground

Decide where to set up your fairground. Pick a place where there's space: a yard, a garage or the local park. You could even pitch a tent! Get an adult's permission first.

2. Come on everybody!

Give your friends plenty of notice. Send invitations to the big day and make sure you know how many are coming, so you can work out how many prizes and how much food you need.

3. Prizes galore!

Everybody expects to win a prize at the fair! Your prizes don't have to be expensive. Buy stickers and treats to hand out and give unwanted books or games as top prizes.

4. Games and stands

It will be hard to recreate a rollercoaster, so stick to games and stands! List the attractions you want and figure out what equipment you need for each one. Here are some ideas...

5. Cake walk game

Set out a number of chairs, as in musical chairs. Each chair has a number on it. Play music while the players walk around the chairs. When the music stops, they sit down. Draw a number out of the hat. The person sitting on that chair wins a cupcake!

6. Knock down game

Collect used drinks cans and wash them out. Stack them up six at a time, with three in the bottom row, two in the middle, and one on the top. Knock the stack down with a tennis ball. All cans down wins a prize!

7. Balls in buckets

For this game, find five large buckets and lots of tennis balls. Line up the buckets and get your friends to throw five balls, one at a time. The object of the game is to land one ball in each bucket!

8. Face painting stall

Is anyone you know artisitc? Persuade a friend or a grown-up to run a face painting stand. Paint simple patterns on cheeks, such as stars or butterflies. Or attempt a cat face with whiskers!

9. Secondhand trading stand

Collect old games, toys, books and clothes that you no longer want. Ask your friends to bring theirs and then trade them at the stall. If anything is left over, give it to charity.

10. Fairground food

Your friends will need refreshments. Include easy-to-make items such as sandwiches, cupcakes and fruit juice. Or you could ask an adult to cook some hot dogs on a barbecue!

Big city trip!

Roxy loves being in a busy city and she's an expert shopper, too!

Unscramble the letters below to find something that Roxy carries with her.

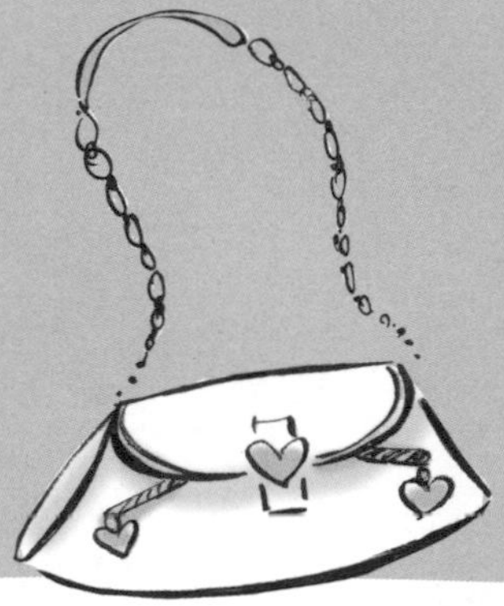

PNEOH

Write the answer here:

....

Find it!

Roxy's scarf is hiding somewhere in this chapter. It looks like this...

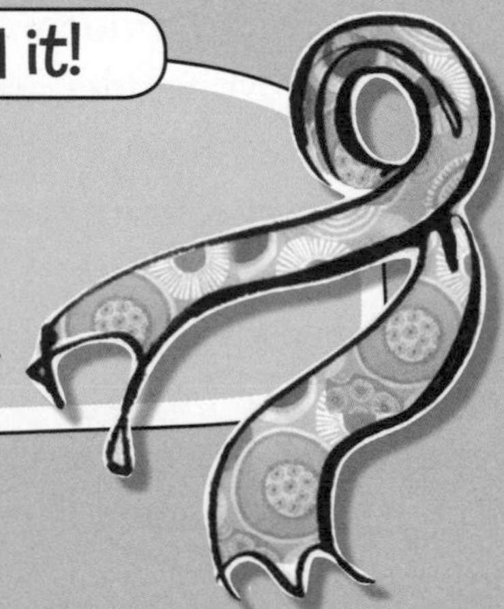

Taylor's trip

The girls hit the big city and Roxy gets to spend the day of her dreams!

PART 5
Continued from page 74...

The girls jumped off the bus and onto a busy city square. Taylor's parents stepped off after them.

"You've got two hours to explore before we go to the museum," Taylor's dad said.

"Thanks Dad," answered Taylor. "We won't go far."

This was Roxy's idea: their first time alone in the big city. Soon the girls were browsing along the store windows but it was all so expensive!

"I think we're in the wrong place for bargains," said Taylor.

"I'll look in the guidebook!" said Milly.

"No, let's just wander around. It's more fun," answered Roxy.

The girls soon found themselves in a maze of alleyways lined with stores and stands, perfect for postcards and souvenirs.

"I'm going to buy my sister Olivia a bracelet with her name on," said Jess.

"That's a good idea. I'll get one for Evie, too," said Roxy.

Taylor overheard their conversation. She had a great idea. To say thanks for cheering her up, she decided to buy ALL the girls matching friendship bracelets.

As Taylor came back from the till, Carla said, "It's time to go. Do we know the way?"

The girls looked blank.

"Oh no. We're lost..." said Milly in a worried voice. "We promised Taylor's dad we wouldn't go very far."

There was a silence, then Jess came to the rescue. "We're not lost. We have a map." She opened Milly's guidebook. "Here's the main square and we're around here..." she paused as she looked for a street sign. Then she grinned, "We're on Friendship Street!"

The girls laughed and cheered up immediately as Jess began to walk confidently in the right direction. As Taylor followed, she smiled secretly to herself. The girls were SO going to love their friendship bracelets...

Continued on page 122...

City scene!

It's exciting being in the big city.
Doodle a bustling cityscape here!

Add a few skyscrapers!

Draw the busy traffic!

Don't forget the stores!

Spot the difference

There are ten tricky differences between these two pictures of the girls shopping. Ring them when you've found them!

A

B

Are you a city girl?

Read these questions and circle your answers.
Check the panel to find out how many points you scored
and discover if you belong in the big city!

1 A friend suggests a city shopping trip. Do you...

A. discover you're already busy

B. flick through your diary to find a free day

C. grab the biggest shopping bag you can find

2 Your best weekend pastime is:

A. mooching around a museum

B. hitting the shops and cafés

C. going for a long walk in the fresh air

3 Your friends want to see a movie in the city. Do you...

A. suggest a trip to a nearby park beforehand

B. suggest you make a whole day of it and go shopping as well

C. suggest going for a pizza after the movie

4 Your best moment in the city is...

A. getting there and feeling the buzz

B. sitting in a café and chatting with your friends

C. getting on the train to go home

5 If you could live anywhere, would it be...

A. in a cute country cottage with a garden

B. in a pretty house on a busy street

C. in a penthouse suite at the top of a skyscraper

Add up your points:

1.	**A** = 1 point	**B** = 2 points	**C** = 3 points
2.	**A** = 2 points	**B** = 3 points	**C** = 1 point
3.	**A** = 1 point	**B** = 3 points	**C** = 2 points
4.	**A** = 3 points	**B** = 2 points	**C** = 1 point
5.	**A** = 1 point	**B** = 2 points	**C** = 3 points

5-8 points

COUNTRY GIRL

The city is fun but it's too big and noisy for you to want to be there all the time. Relax in the country air!

9-11 points

ANYWHERE GOES

You love the countryside but you love cities, too! You'll be happy anywhere you can find good friends!

12-15 points

CITY LOVER

The city is the place for you. You love the noise, you love the people and the stores are amazing!

Puzzle parade

Which shadow exactly matches this picture of Roxy?

Roxy is shopping for earrings. Match up these earrings into pairs.

Meeting mix up!

The girls have arranged to meet up but Roxy is waiting in the wrong place. Can you take the other girls to find her?

Puzzle parade

Roxy and Taylor are thirsty. Which line takes them to the café?

Circle the words that CAN'T be made out of the letters in the word SHOPAHOLIC.

POSH

LOLLIPOP

POLISH

HELLO

PILLOW

SPILL

OPAL

Can you find three differences between these pictures of Roxy's shoes?

1

2

Draw Roxy!

Copy Roxy's picture into the grid, square by square.

ROXY'S FASHION TIP
A cool jacket looks great with jeans and dresses, too!

Fill it in!

What do YOU wear with jeans?

....

....

Shopping mall maze

This shopping mall is SO huge. The girls split up to explore. Look at the key and then take the right pair of girls to the right store. Now take them all to the café for an ice cream!

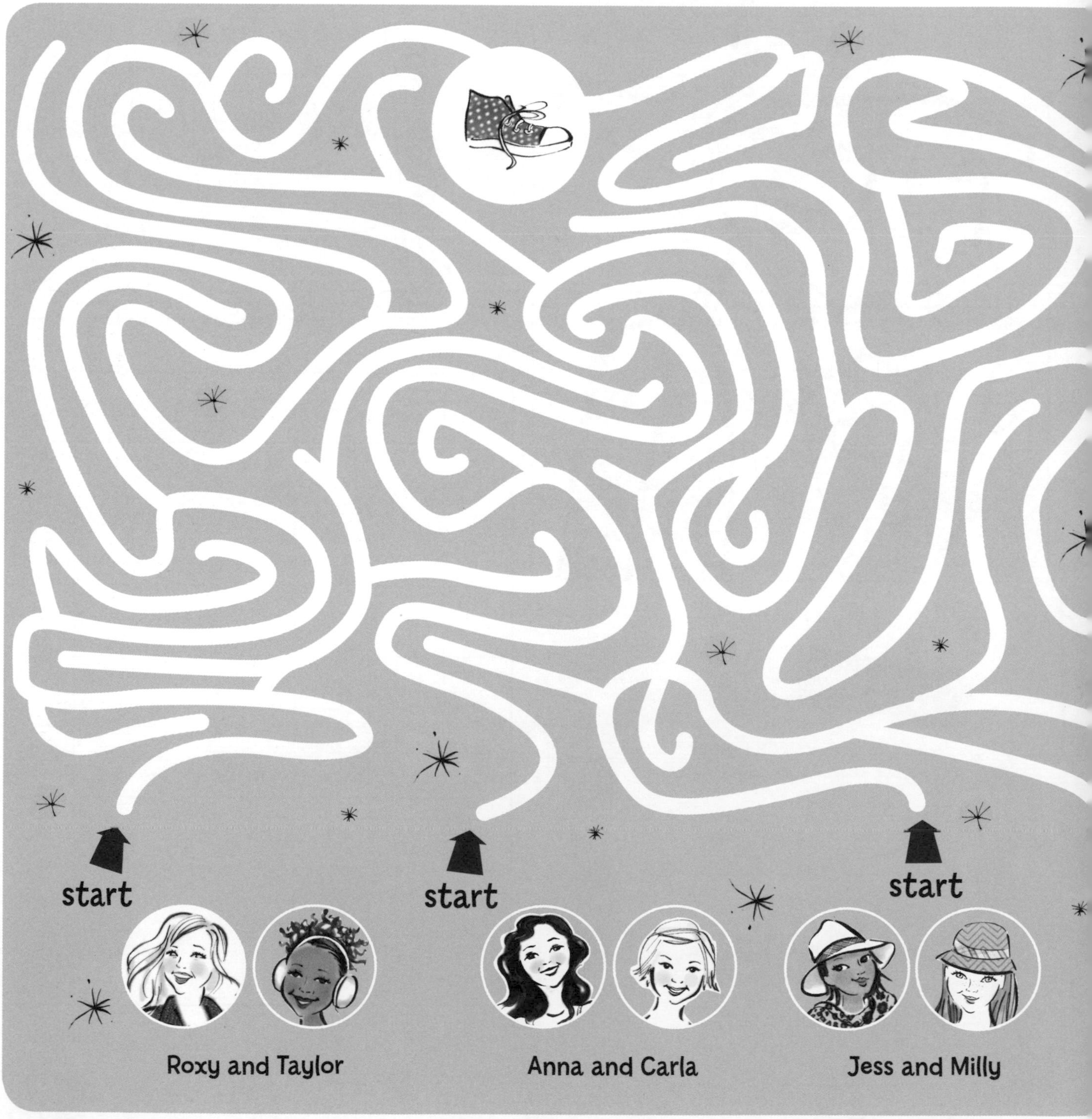

KEY

Roxy and Taylor

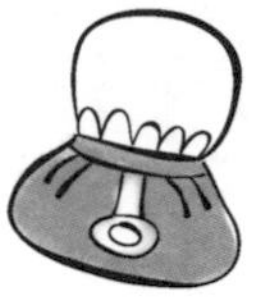
Anna and Carla

Jess and Milly

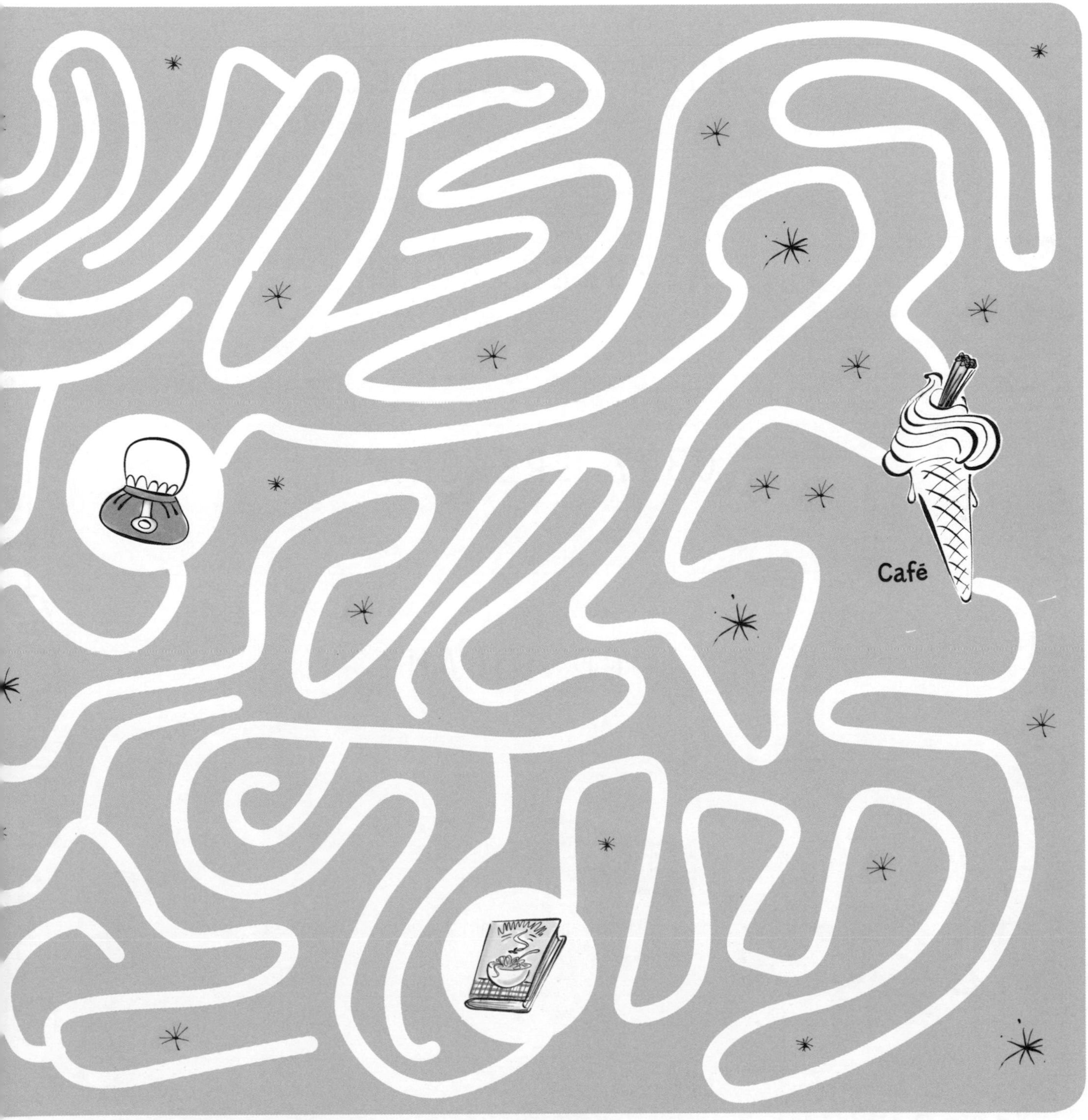

If your thing is bling...

The words below are all mixed up. Unscramble them to find four different "bling" things!
Clue: they are all made of precious materials.

MIODAND LACKNECE

IAPPSRHE AAITR

UBRY SREAGRIN

LOGD HICAN

Fill it in!

What sparkly thing would YOU love to own?

....

....

Picture puzzle

Solve this puzzle to make a picture in the grid. Here's how: the numbers tell you how many squares to shade in each row or column. For instance, if the number clue is **2 1** there are **2** shaded blocks followed by at least one space, then **1** shaded block in that row or column. When you've finished, a picture of a letter will be revealed!

Hint: Shade five squares in this column!

	5	1 1	1 1	2 1	1
4					
1 1					
3					
1 1					
1 1					■

We've done one for you already!

When you've revealed the letter, whose name begins with it?

Write it here:

....

Puzzle parade

Which picture of Roxy is the odd one out?

Roxy and Jess decide to buy friendship bracelets for their sisters. Can you put the beads in the right order to spell out the sisters' names? Clue: look back at page 98 if you're not sure...

Roxy's sister

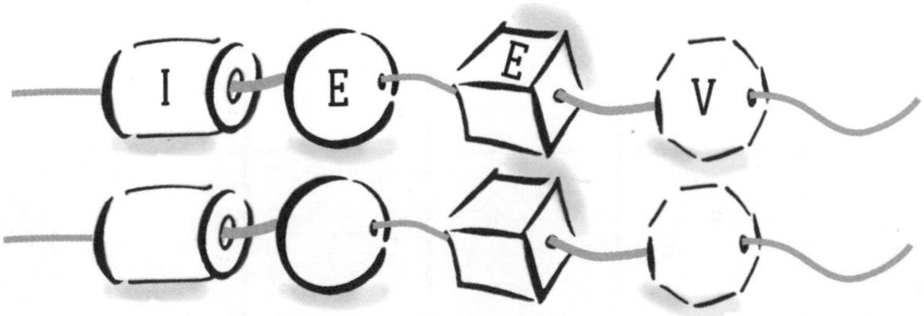

Jess's sister

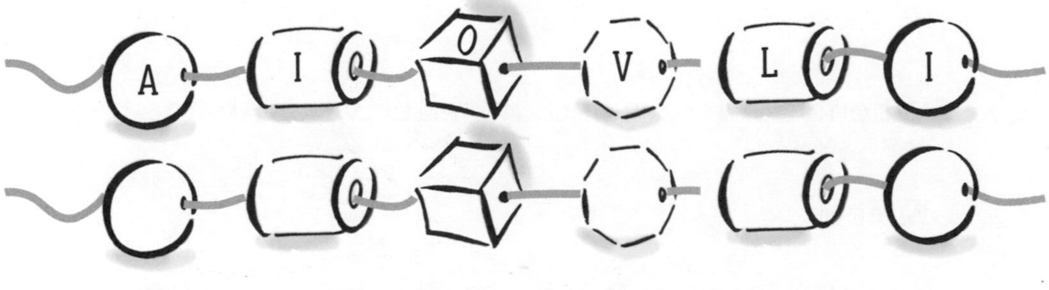

Roxy's top fashion

Add pretty shades and patterns to make outfits for Roxy to wear on her trip.

Do the shorts match the top?

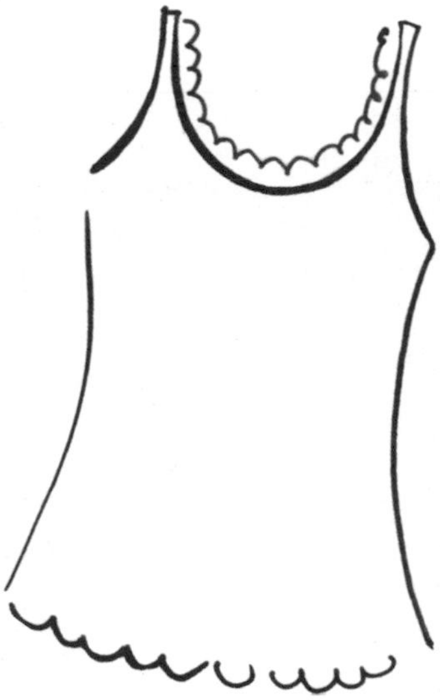

Draw sparkles on the shoes!

See the sights!

On a day trip to the city, you don't want to go home without seeing at least one major tourist attraction. But which one would YOU choose? Answer the questions and follow the arrows to find out!

start

After reading your guidebook, do you head straight for the old part of the city?

Every time

Not this time

On your way, do you watch for famous landmarks?

Definitely!

Sounds dull!

You see the city flag. Do you explain to your friends what the pictures mean?

Yep, that's me!

Not me!

You love every bit of the city, you're in a spin! What do you do?

Pick a place and go there...

Don't know, can't decide!

Do you love the city's open spaces best, such as the squares and parks?

Not really

Of course

Do you sit in a café and check the map?

Nope. Keep walking...

Good plan!

Do you sit for ages, grab a bite to eat and watch the people go by?

No fun!

Best fun!

Are you desperate to see paintings by the city's most famous artist?

Yes! / No...

When you go past interesting buildings, do you look them up in your guidebook straight away?

Love to! / Later...

When you get home, do you want to boast about the one crazy thing you did?

Maybe? / That's so true!

Do you travel on an tourist bus so you can see the sights as you go?

Sounds great! / I'm walking!

Do you wonder what the city people do to relax on weekends?

Yep! / Nope

MUSEUM

You love history and want to find out more about this great city. Head for the museum. You'll lose yourself for hours!

BOTANICAL GARDENS

You're in the middle of a city but you love quiet, too. Walk in the gardens for a breath of fresh air!

TALLEST TOWER

You're so thrilled by being in the big city that you want to see it ALL. Race to the top of the tallest building for an amazing view!

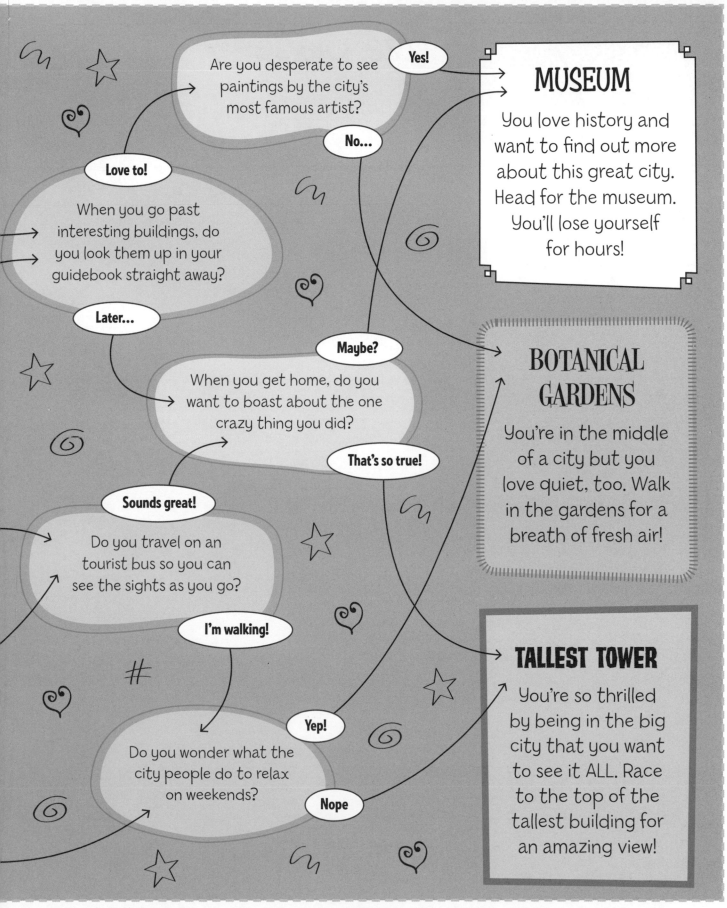

Pizza place

The girls stop at a pizza place for lunch.
Doodle a yummy pizza here!

Is it mega-meaty?

Is it a veggie feast?

Is it a special recipe?

Puzzle parade

Find the vehicles hidden in these sentences.
The first one is done for you.

1. Roxy's **plan e**ventually worked: the girls agreed to go shopping!
2. The cabins were decorated with flowers in a tub, usually placed by the front door.
3. Anna announced that the weather report had forecast rain for tomorrow.
4. The girls remembered to buy birthday cards for Taylor's mother.

It's time for the girls to head back to Lake Truly.
Help them find their way!

TOP 10 TIPS for terrific travel games!

Bored on the bus? Having a tedious time on the train? Play one of these fun travel games and you'll soon be at your destination!

1. Magazine hunt

Give each player a few magazines and a list of ten items to find, such as a bag, a flower, a city scene etc. See who can flick through and spot all ten first!

2. Celebrity style

Take turns to pretend to be a well-known celebrity but don't tell the others who you are. The other players ask questions, to which the 'celebrity' can only answer yes or no. The first person to guess the celebrity's identity is the winner.

3. Hum it!

Take it in turns to hum a well-known song. The other players have to guess what you're humming. It's easy and it's also a lot of fun!

4. Alphabet animals

Go through the alphabet taking turns to name animals starting with each letter. And when you've done animals, you could do girls' names or capital cities or countries... the list is endless!

5. License plate words

This game is ideal for a drive. Take turns to spot a car license plate (preferrably the one right in front) and think of a word that uses the letters on the license plate but in the right order. Tricky!

6. Tell me a story

It can be a lot of fun making up stories, especially if you do it together. One person starts the story, no longer than a few sentences. Take turns to be the storyteller and see where you end up!

7. What's my job?

This game is great for trains. Each player has to mime an action to do with a particular job and the other players have to guess what it is!

8. Counting queens

Each player chooses an object to count that you can easily see out of the window, such as blue cars, restaurants, signposts etc. Give everyone two minutes to count as many of their objects as possible. The biggest number wins!

9. In my bag...

The first player says, "In my bag I packed..." and then lists an item (it can be made up!). The second player then repeats the sentence but adds an item of her own. Each player takes it in turns, adding an item each time. Keep going for as long as you can!

10. And lastly...

You can't go on a trip without playing I-Spy, the best travel game ever! You know what to do...

The end of the adventure!

It's the last day of the trip and Jess takes the girls on a hike. Unscramble the letters below to find something else that Jess loves doing in her spare time...

NICCGYL

Write the answer here:

....

Find it!

Jess's skateboard is hidden somewhere in this chapter. It looks like this...

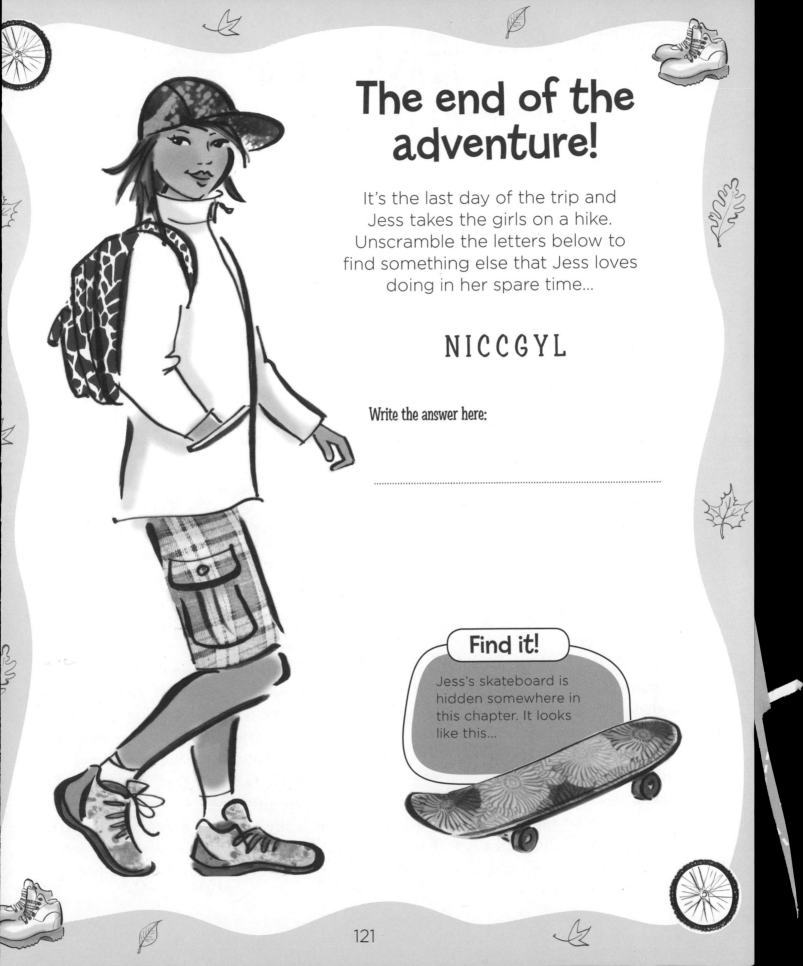

Taylor's trip

PART 6
Continued from page 98...

It's the last day of the trip and it's Jess's turn to plan the day as the girls say goodbye to Lake Truly...

It was a bright, breezy day and the girls walked quickly, admiring the beautiful lake with the boats skipping over the water. Jess was taking them on a hike around Lake Truly and it wasn't long before they reached their picnic spot. As they ate, the girls began to chat about their trip.

"My best bit was getting lost in the city," said Roxy excitedly.

"Except we didn't really get lost, thanks to Jess and the map!" said Milly.

"I loved the water park and the horse riding," said Anna. "They were both really fun."

"The fair was cool too though, especially as I was the surprise winner of the dance competition!" Roxy laughed.

"Yep," said Jess. "And today is great too. We've walked round half the lake already! What about you, Taylor?"

Taylor hesitated. In fact, she'd been quiet throughout the whole conversation.

"Are you still feeling sad about the dance classes, Taylor?" said Anna kindly.

Taylor shook her head and beamed a big smile. "I was just thinking... if I'd gone to dance classes every day, I wouldn't have been able to do all these other great things. So to say thank you, I've got you all a present."

Taylor shuffled through her backpack, then handed out a bracelet to each friend. "They're all the same," she said, "They're to remind us of our trip!"

Anna looked at the beaded bracelet in her hand. Letters on the beads spelt out two words: TRULY FRIENDS.

"Taylor, that's so sweet!" Anna exclaimed. "Thanks so much!"

"Yes, thanks, Taylor!" they all agreed.

"Come on everyone, don't forget it's barbecue night back at the cabin. We don't want to miss out on the end to a TRULY fantastic day!" Jess laughed.

The girls gave each other a huge hug. It really had been a *truly* amazing trip...

The End!

In the bag!

What does Jess carry in her backpack? Doodle it!

Is it spare socks?

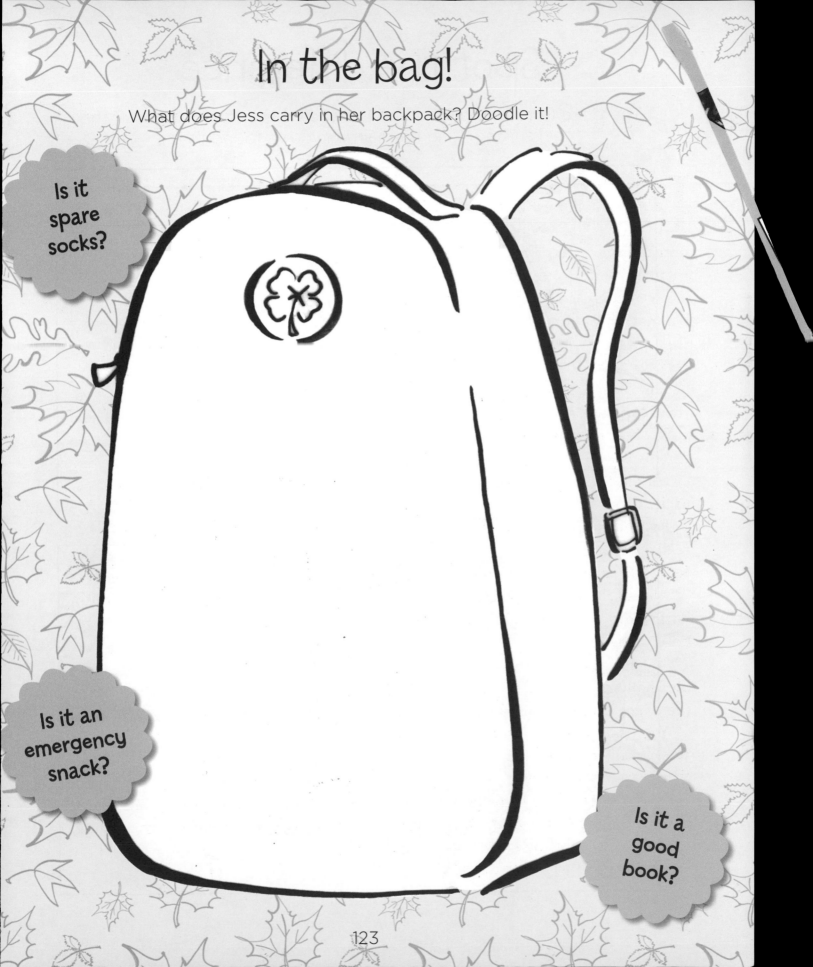

Is it an emergency snack?

Is it a good book?

Spot the difference

There are ten tricky differences between these two pictures of the girls hiking. Ring them when you've found them!

A

B

Wild weather quiz!

Get your best friend to do this weather quiz with you. If you don't know the answers, have a guess. Check the back of the book to see how many you got right!

1. What is a tornado?
a) a spinning column of wind
b) a heavy rainstorm
c) a big black cloud

☐ YOU ☐ YOUR BEST FRIEND

2. What is a haboob?
a) a really huge puddle
b) a sandstorm in a desert
c) a massive snow drift

☐ YOU ☐ YOUR BEST FRIEND

3. What is the word "cirrus" used to describe?
a) a type of raindrop
b) a type of snowflake
c) a type of cloud

☐ YOU ☐ YOUR BEST FRIEND

4. What comes first in a storm, thunder or lightning?
a) thunder
b) lightning
c) always both together

☐ YOU ☐ YOUR BEST FRIEND

5. What is a hurricane?
a) a huge storm that starts at night
b) a huge storm that starts at sea
c) a huge storm that starts in a hurry

☐ YOU ☐ YOUR BEST FRIEND

6. What is the name for tiny balls of ice that fall like rain?
a) icicles
b) grit
c) hail

☐ YOU ☐ YOUR BEST FRIEND

7. Which of these is included in the rainbow?
a) maroon
b) violet
c) lilac

☐ YOU ☐ YOUR BEST FRIEND

8. Are snowflakes symmetrical?
a) yes
b) no
c) sometimes

☐ YOU ☐ YOUR BEST FRIEND

9. Which of these ISN'T a type of cloud?
a) nimbus
b) tumnus
c) cumulus

☐ YOU ☐ YOUR BEST FRIEND

10. Is it possible to see a double rainbow?
a) yes
b) no
c) only on a really hot day

☐ YOU
☐ YOUR BEST FRIEND

Puzzle parade

Which picture of Jess is the odd one out?

1

2

3

Jess is planning the route. She works out the following:

It's 1 hour and 30 minutes walk to the picnic spot.

The girls want to break for 30 minutes for lunch.

Then it's a 1 hour and 15 minutes around the lake and back to the resort.

If they stop for two extra breaks at 15 minutes each, how long does the whole hike take?

Write the answer here

Draw Jess!

Copy Jess's picture into the grid, square by square.

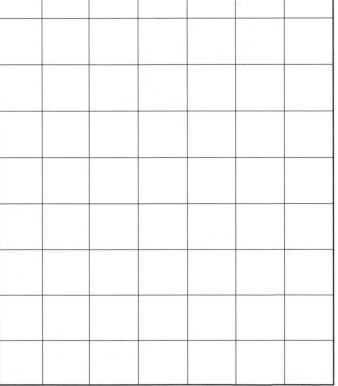

JESS'S FASHION TIP
A fun backpack is cool for school and out of school, too!

Fill it in!

What does YOUR backpack look like?

....

....

Follow the trail

This is a game for two players. Start at number one. Take turns to throw a die and move around the board. Use coins or small charms as counters and follow the key opposite. Don't get lost!

Key

If you land on a signpost, you're on the right trail! Follow the path up to the higher square.

If you land on a map, move forward three squares.

If you land on a tree, you're lost! Follow the path down to the square below.

If you land on a sandwich, miss a turn as you stop for a picnic!

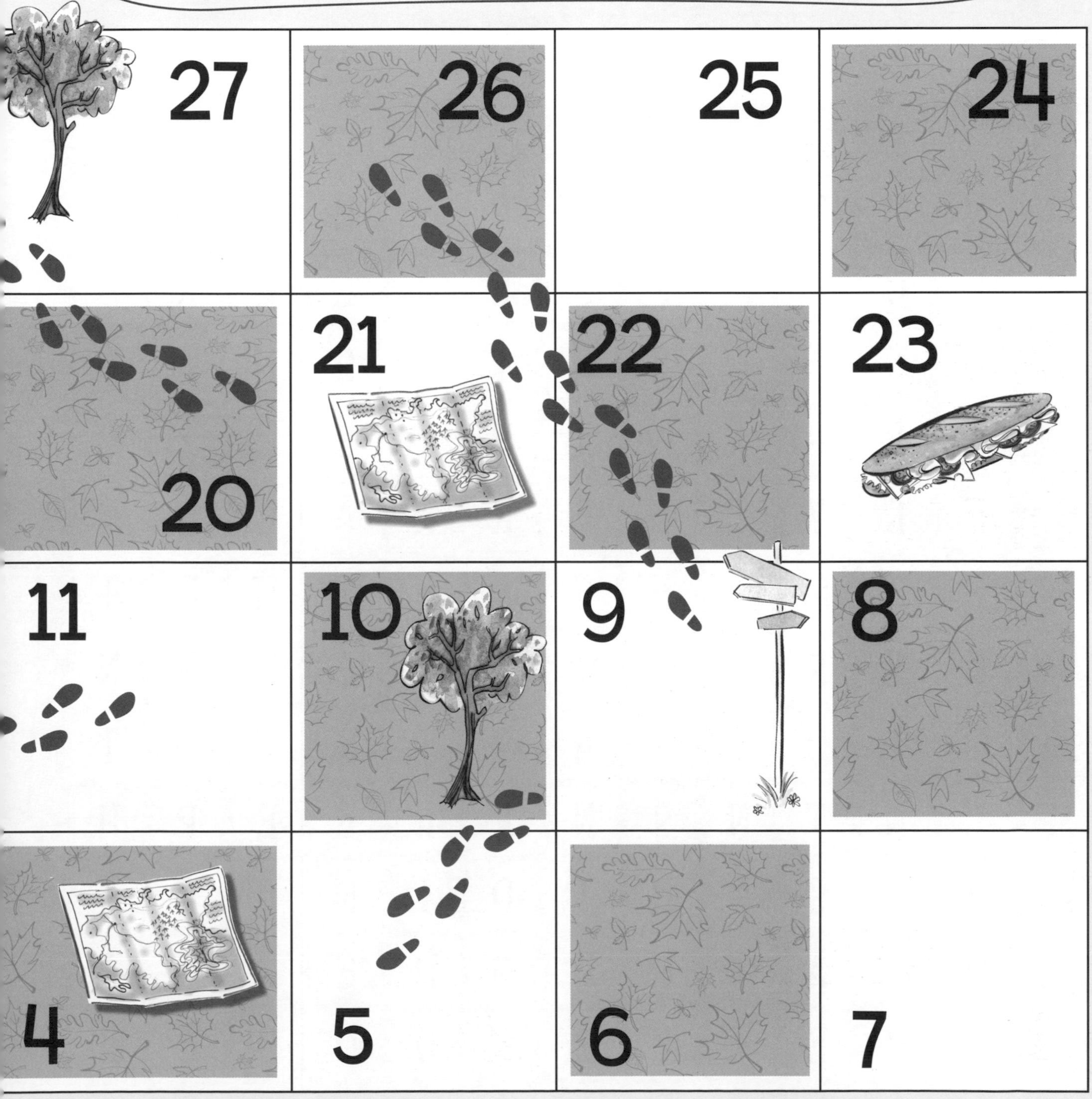

Weather words

Find the weather words in the grid. Look up, down, backward, across and diagonally.

Word list

- breeze
- cloud
- hail
- ice
- lightning
- rainbow
- raindrops
- storm
- sun
- thunder
- snowflakes
- wind

B	S	T	O	Z	E	P	Y	H	E	T	K
E	U	N	M	P	S	E	Z	E	E	R	B
B	N	W	O	B	N	I	A	R	H	A	F
R	E	G	A	W	K	E	Y	B	H	I	G
E	L	Y	T	L	F	K	R	A	L	N	N
Z	A	M	I	N	E	L	H	T	H	D	I
O	X	R	W	C	W	T	A	E	Z	R	N
T	I	O	I	I	A	S	I	K	V	O	T
S	N	T	N	S	N	E	L	E	E	P	H
A	L	S	G	H	T	D	I	N	G	S	G
D	I	A	T	H	U	N	D	E	R	N	I
I	C	E	I	Y	E	D	U	O	L	C	L

Super sudoku!

This sudoku is super tricky. You have to get all the numbers from 1 to 9 in the right place in every 3 x 3 square, row and column. Enjoy!

6		8				5		1
	9	7		8	5	3		
	4		3	6	9		2	
4	5		9				6	
			2	3	8			
	1				6		7	3
	8		6		7		5	
		9	8	2	4	1	3	
		1				6		4

Getting stuck?

Here are some clues to get you started:

* The bottom right square is missing a number 8. There's only one place it could go...
* The second column in from the right is missing a number 1. Where could you put it?
* The top right square is missing a number 6. Where does it go? Look carefully...

Puzzle parade

Which shadow exactly matches this picture of Jess?

Which one of Jess's friends is hiding in this puzzle picture?

Write her name here:

____

Jess's top fashion

Add pretty shades and patterns to make an outfit for Jess to wear on her trip.

Does she have patterns on her jeans?

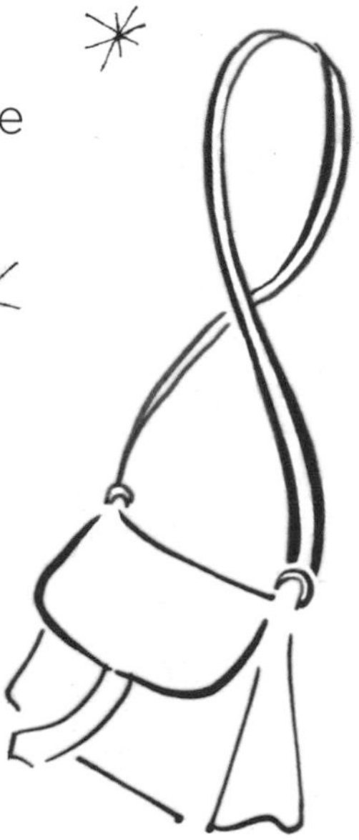

Draw a logo on her bag!

Does the jacket have pockets?

Woodland walk

You're hiking through a forest.
What do you see? Doodle it!

Is it a cute animal?

Is it a pretty flower?

Is it the perfect picnic spot?

Puzzle parade

Jess loves sports and she loves speed and excitement. How many speedy sports can you think of? Here's an easy one to start you off...

Skateboarding

The girls are spotting different types of trees on their walk. Check off each leaf when you find it below.

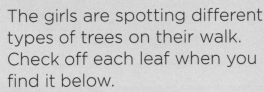

Jess's diary

Jess wants to rate all the things the girls did on their trip. How would YOU rate each one? Circle a number for each activity. 1 = OK and 5 = Amazing.

MY TRIP

We're going home tomorrow. Boo! But here's what I think of all the things we did on our trip to Lake Truly.

SUNDAY: WATER PARK

Anna took us to the water park where we swam and played on the slides.

Rate: 1 2 3 4 5

MONDAY: HORSE RIDING

Carla took us horse riding. My horse was called Duke. He was awesome.

Rate: 1 2 3 4 5

TUESDAY: THE FAIR

Milly suggested we go to the fair. It was loads of fun.

Rate: 1 2 3 4 5

WEDNESDAY: CITY TRIP

Roxy loves shopping so we went to the city. We did SO much sightseeing.

Rate: 1 2 3 4 5

THURSDAY: HIKING

I took the girls on a hike around the lake. It was a challenge and we made it!

Rate: 1 2 3 4 5

Fill it in!

What's YOUR best activity? Rate it!

....

TOP 10 TIPS for going on an adventure!

Here are some activities you can try that will get you out in the great outdoors... plus some top tips for making the most of them!

1. Before you set out

Adventures are lots of fun! But always get the permission of an adult before you go anywhere and follow their rules. Whoever you're with, make sure that someone else knows where you're planning to go and roughly what time you'll be back.

2. Go hiking...

The easiest way to get outdoors is to go hiking. If you live near the countryside, there are probably lots of places nearby where you can walk. If you live in a city, find your nearest park!

3. ... or go biking

If you love the feeling of freedom and you want to go a bit farther than your feet will carry you, then get on your bike! Look for cycle paths in your local area and plan a ride with friends.

4. Build a camp

Head for a local forest where you can test your survival skills! Build a camp from branches and foliage or light a campfire. (Only do this if an adult is with you who knows how to light fires safely.)

5. Play geocache

Geocaching is a hide and seek treasure hunting game played outdoors with a GPS device. You explore an area to find 'caches', which sometimes contain little presents. You can also leave your own present behind, too!

6. Go on a night walk

Exploring by night has its own special atmosphere. Nocturnal animals are awake, noises seem louder and everything looks different by moonlight. Many parks and wildlife groups run night walks, so why not join one?

7. Do something fun!

And if that's not enough, you could always ask an adult to let you do something exciting you've always wanted to do, such as get up early and watch the sun rise or fly a kite on a windy hilltop!

8. Map it out

Whatever activity you're doing, before you set out you have to know where you're going! Plan your route on a map and estimate how long you're going to be out. And take the map with you!

9. Pack a snack

It's easy to get tired and hungry if you're outside all day so take plenty of snacks and drinks with you. High energy foods, such as bananas or chocolate, are good and will get you back on track.

10. Saftey tips

If you're hiking, biking, or on any other kind of outdoor adventure, it's always a good idea to take a first aid kit and a phone in case of emergencies. And don't forget to make sure the phone is charged up!

Answers to puzzles

Page 6
BEST FRIENDS

Taylor's backpack can be found on page 12.

Page 8
Picture 3

LAKE is the word to do with Taylor's trip.

Page 10

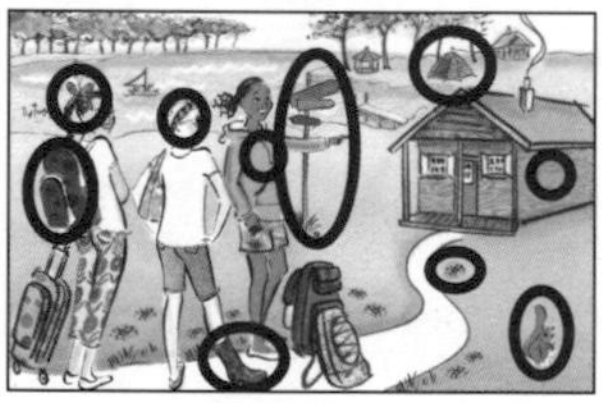

Page 12

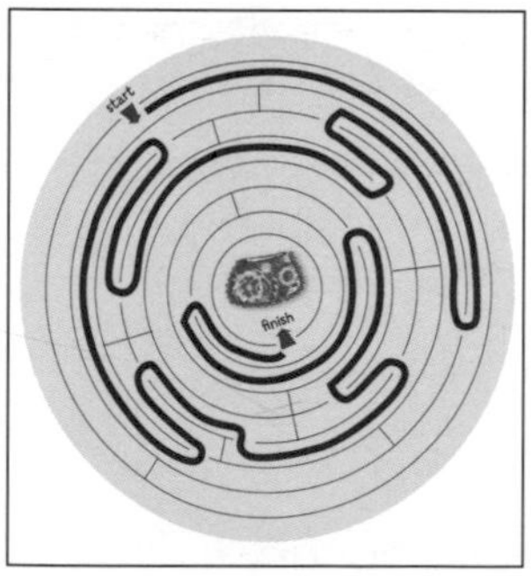

Page 13
Shadow 2

Taylor loves DANCING.

Page 14

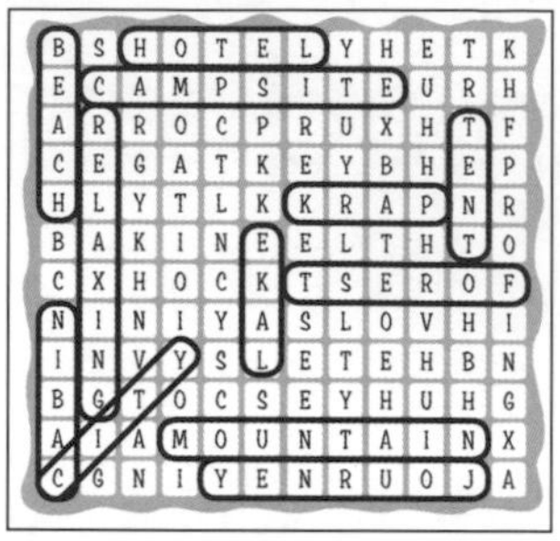

Pages 16-17

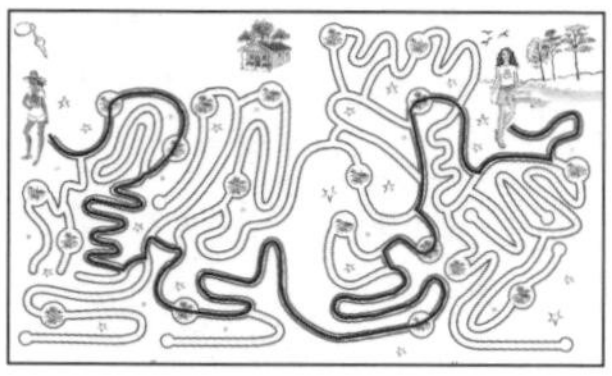

Page 19
Hairband C

4 hours

Page 23
Guitars 2 and 4

From the letters in the words LAKE TRULY, you can make: eat, leak, let, rake, rat, rule, rut, take, tale, tall, tea, teak, tear, tell, true, yell; and more!

Page 25
SWIMMING BAG

Anna's best swimsuit can be found on page 37.

Page 28

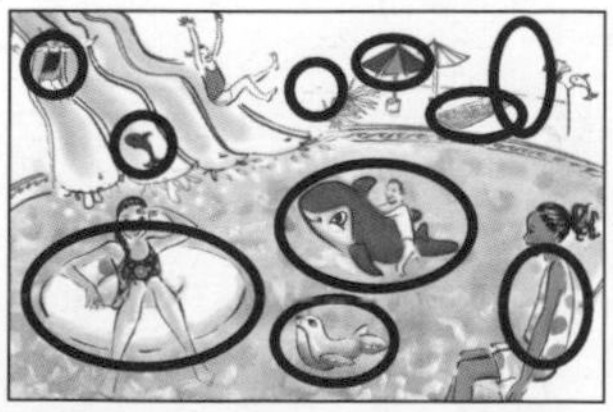

Page 30
Pictures 1 and 3 are the same.

SPLASH, SPLAT, SWIPE, WALK and WHISK can't be made our of the letters in WATER PARKS.

Page 31

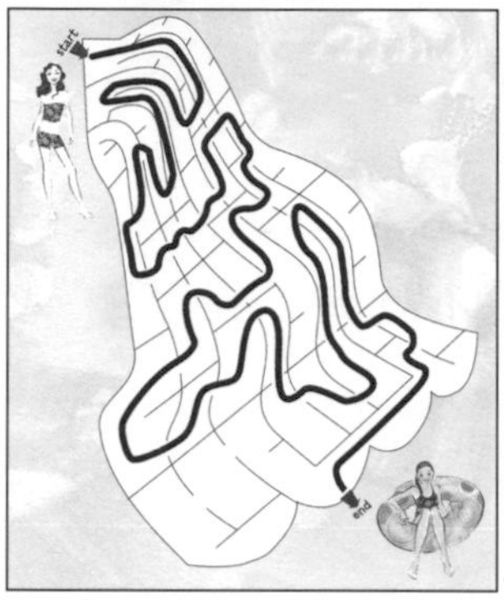

Page 32
canoeing
diving
kite surfing
rowing
sailing
surfing
swimming
synchronized swimming
water polo
waterskiing
water volleyball
windsurfing

3 hours and 30 minutes

Page 36
Anna's secret message reads: LEARNING TO SWIM KEEPS YOU SAFE IN THE WATER

Page 37
Anna's hairbrush, goggles and spare shorts are missing.

Page 38
Shadow 3

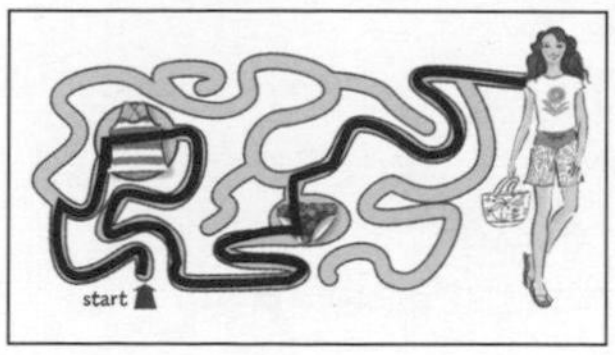

Page 44
Here are a few girls' names beginning with "A" to start you off... Alexandra, Amelia, Alice, Antonia, Asha...

Anna got the most points.

Page 45
1. True; 2. False; 3. True; 4. True; 5. False; 6. False; 7. False: you use a puck; 8. True; 9. True; 10. False: a martial art is one which involves combat; 11. True; 12. False: BMX riding began in the 1960s; 13. False: badminton is played with a shuttlecock; 14. True; 15. False; 16. True; 17. True; 18. True; 19. False: Michael Phelps is a famous swimmer; 20. False: the Olympics are held once every four years.

Page 47
Line 3

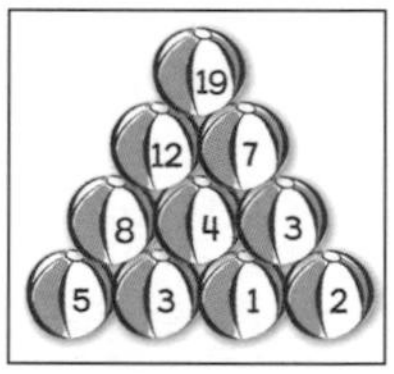

SWIMSUITS

Page 49
PHOTO OF HER HORSE

Carla's riding hat can be found on page 56.

Page 52

Page 54
Shadow 3

BLACK
CHESTNUT
PIEBALD
BAY

Page 55

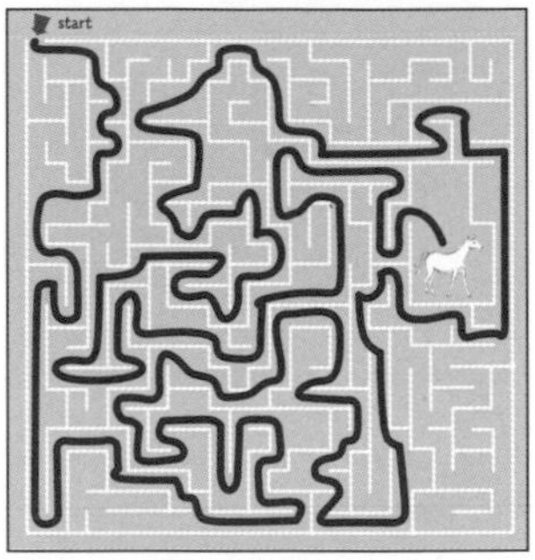

Page 56

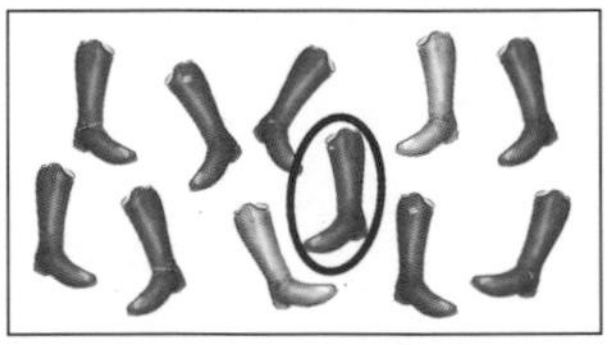

Page 58

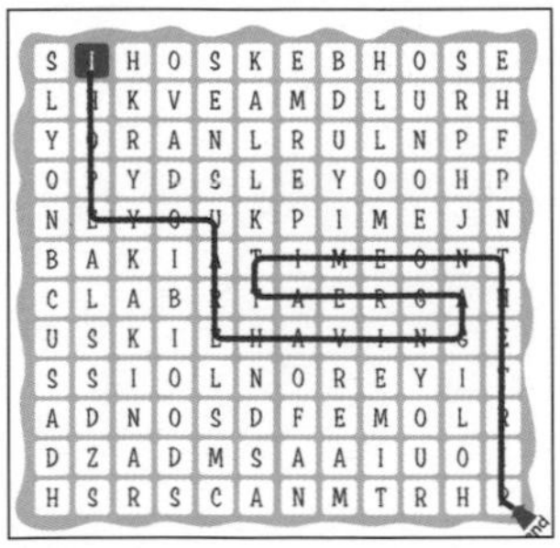

Page 59

Taylor / Stella / Chestnut
Milly / Rocket / Bay
Roxy / Jolly / Piebald
Anna / Jensen / Palomino
Jess / Duke / Black

Pages 60-61

1st round = 14 points
2nd round = 18 points
3rd round = 22 points
4th round = 24 points
5th round = 20 points
TOTAL = 98 points

Page 62

15 buckets
18 horseshoes

Picture 3

Pages 64-65

Page 68

From the letters in the words RIDING STABLES, you can make: bale, bar, blade, bless, bride, din, grab, less, rib, rid, ring, stab, star, steal, tar; and more!

Line B

Page 71

JOLLY
ROCKET
STELLA
DUKE
JENSEN

Page 73

HOT DOG WITH KETCHUP

Milly's sun hat can be found on page 91.

Page 76

Page 78

Picture 1

FERRIS WHEEL

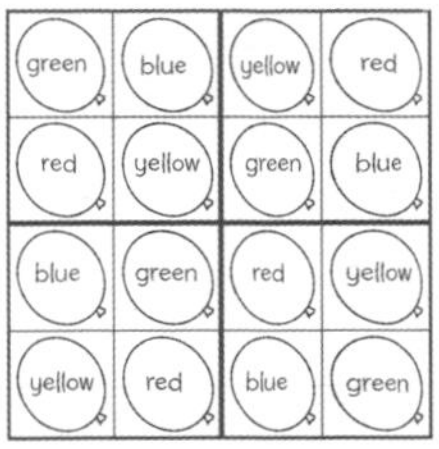

Page 79

Page 80

Shadow 3

Milly can use tokens 12, 9 and 4.

Pages 82-83

Milly's secret message reads: WE ARE GOING TO THE GHOST TRAIN NEXT. CAN YOU KEEP A SECRET? ROXY IS FEELING SCARED!

Page 84

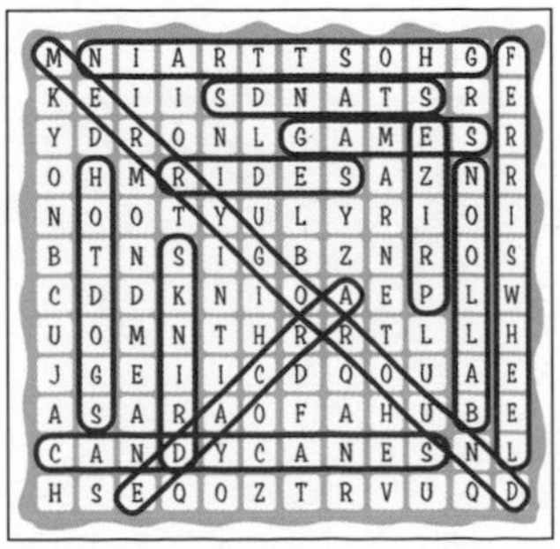

Page 85

Tent 4 is the correct match.

Page 86

Here are a few girls' names beginning with "M" to start you off: Madeline, Maria, May, Mia, Molly...

Page 90

The words are:
PHOTO
GIRLS
CABIN
FOOD
FAIR
FRIENDS
PARK

When the missing letters are rearranged, they spell COOKING.

Hot dogs 1 and 4

Page 93

In order, the paragraphs are 4th, 3rd, 1st, 2nd.

Page 95

The pairs are:
1 and 5
2 and 3
4 and 6

Line B

Page 97

PHONE

Roxy's scarf can be found on page 101.

Page 100

Page 102
Shadow 3

The pairs are: A and D; B and G; C and F; E and H.

Page 103

Page 104
Line B

LOLLIPOP, HELLO, PILLOW AND SPILL can't be made out of the letters in the word SHOPAHOLIC.

Page 106-107

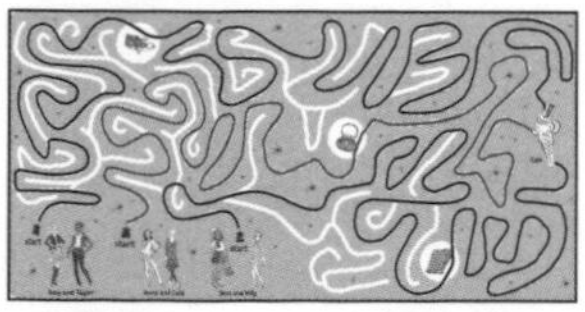

Page 108
DIAMOND NECKLACE
SAPPHIRE TIARA
RUBY EARRINGS
GOLD CHAIN

Page 109

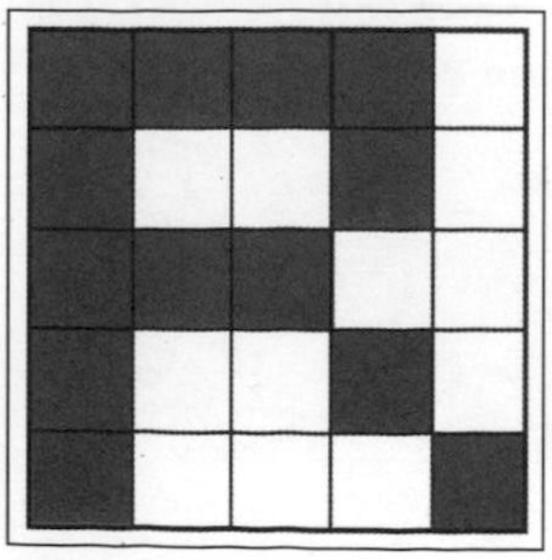

Page 110
Picture 3

Evie
Olivia

Page 116
Yes, the girls make it on time

2 and 3 are exactly the same

Page 119
1. Roxy's **plan e**ventually worked: the girls agreed to go shopping!

2. The **cab**ins were decorated with flowers in a tu**b, us**ually by the front door.

3. Anna announced that the weather report had forecas**t rain** for tomorrow.

4. The girls remembered to buy birthday **car**ds for Taylor's mother.

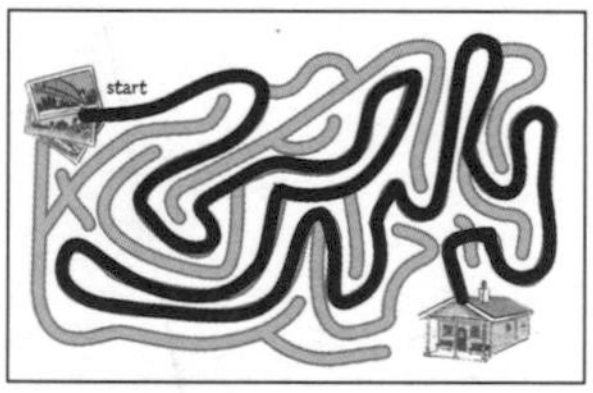

Page 121
CYCLING

Jess's skateboard can be found on page 137.

Page 124

Page 125
1a; 2b; 3c; 4b; 5b; 6c; 7b; 8a; 9b; 10a

Page 126
Picture 2

3 hours and 45 minutes

Page 127

Page 128
Backpacks 3 and 4

MOUNTAIN

Page 132

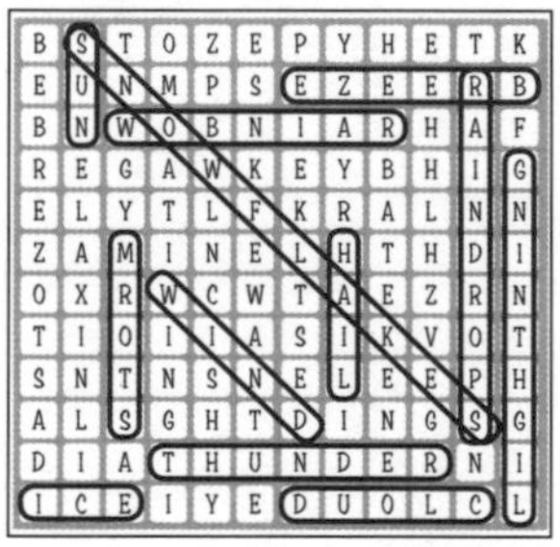

Page 133

6	3	8	7	4	2	5	9	1
2	9	7	1	8	5	3	4	6
1	4	5	3	6	9	7	2	8
4	5	3	9	7	1	8	6	2
9	7	6	2	3	8	4	1	5
8	1	2	4	5	6	9	7	3
3	8	4	6	1	7	2	5	9
5	6	9	8	2	4	1	3	7
7	2	1	5	9	3	6	8	4

Page 134
Shadow 3

Milly

Page 137
BMXing
horse riding
mountain biking
motor racing
rafting
rollerblading
skateboarding
skiing
snowboarding
surfing

Page 139
The pairs are:
1 and 6
2 and 4
3 and 5

From the letters in the words FRIENDS FOREVER, you can make:
drive, end, ever, feed, fever, five, for, friend, if, need, reed, reef, rod, seed, send, verse; and more!